the complete guide to

SELLING
YOUR
BUSINESS

the complete guide to

SELLING
YOUR
BUSINESS

PAUL SPERRY & BEATRICE H MITCHELL

INSTITUTE OF DIRECTORS

KOGAN
PAGE

This book provides an overview of the subject of mergers and acquisitions. It is presented with the understanding that neither the authors nor the publisher are engaged in rendering legal or accounting services. If legal, tax or accounting, or other expert assistance is required, the services of a competent professional should be sought.

For the sake of simplicity, the authors have used 'he' to stand for 'he or she' throughout this book.

First published in the USA by Upstart Publishing Company, Inc, Dover, New Hampshire 03820 in 1992

This UK edition published by Kogan Page in 1999

Kogan Page Limited
120 Pentonville Road
London N1 9JN, UK

Kogan Page Limited
163 Central Avenue, Suite 4
Dover NH 03820, USA

The Institute of Directors accepts no responsibility for the opinions expressed by the author of this publication. Readers should consult their advisors before acting on any of the issues raised.

British Library Cataloguing in Publication Data

A CIP record for this book is available from the British Library.

ISBN 0 7494 2904 6

Typeset by JS Typesetting, Wellingborough, Northants
Printed and bound in Great Britain by Clays Ltd, St Ives plc

'There is no man who is not in some degree a merchant; who has not something to buy or something to sell.'

Samuel Johnson

ABOUT THE AUTHORS

Paul Sperry and Beatrice Mitchell are principals in the New York-based investment banking firm of Sperry, Mitchell & Company, which specializes in representing small to medium-sized private companies seeking a sale or merger. The two have over 40 years of collective experience in the merger and acquisition fields, mostly concentrating on transactions involving middle-market companies.

Paul S Sperry received his BA from Trinity College and an MA from Columbia University. Prior to establishing Sperry, Mitchell & Co, he was President of another small investment bank in New York. He is on the board of a number of private companies and non-profit organizations.

Beatrice H Mitchell received her BA from Yale University and an MBA from Columbia. She has had significant prior experience in both the banking and advertising fields. Ms Mitchell is on the board of numerous non-profit and community organizations.

Both are recognized experts in the field of mergers and acquisitions, and are frequent participants and featured speakers at M&A seminars, trade associations and industry conferences. Ms Mitchell is a regular lecturer at Columbia University Business School.

Both Mr Sperry and Ms Mitchell have been widely quoted by the press, most recently in *The Wall Street Journal*, *USA Today*, *Acquisitions Monthly*, and *CNN Moneyline*, and on National Public Radio. They are also frequent contributors to business and academic publications.

For Sarah, William and Frances:
our beloved children

Contents

Introduction

Recently, we were involved in the sale of a medium-sized distributor of pneumatic tools. The company had been run very successfully for over 20 years by its two owners. While both enjoyed working and were in good health, they had reached the point in life where they wanted to work less hard, take more time off and enjoy the fruits of their labour.

Though both men had families, none of their children worked in the company, nor did any of them have any interest in joining. The company had a capable second tier of management, but there was no one who could really run the business besides the two owners. After much consideration, both men decided that the only sensible alternative open to them was to sell.

Having arrived at the decision to sell, the owners next had the difficult task of figuring out how to go about it. They did not want to talk to their competitors, for obvious concerns of confidentiality. They had some vague ideas as to other companies that might have an interest, but they had no idea how to approach them.

By chance, we met both owners at a social function, and they told us of their dilemma. A number of conversations and meetings ensued, and we were retained to handle the sale of their business. The search and negotiation process took six months, during which time both owners were exposed to numerous potential acquirers offering varying types of transactions. The company was eventually sold to two wealthy private investors, one of whom wanted to run the business. After a two-month transitional period, both clients retired completely from the business, satisfying one of their original goals.

Over lunch a few weeks after the transaction was completed, one of the owners remarked to us that he had no idea what he was getting into when he first addressed the idea of selling. Though he had been a capable businessman who had built a successful company, he felt totally unprepared as to what to expect in selling his company. He did not know what a Letter of Intent was, or what to look for in a Purchase Agreement. He did not even know where to get good, competent advice on these matters. Our client went on to suggest that it would have been quite helpful if he had a guide at the beginning of the process that would have educated and prepared him for what was to follow.

That conversation was the genesis of this book. As intermediaries dealing with private company owners on a daily basis, we have come to realize that very few business owners have a proper understanding of matters relating to mergers and acquisitions.

This book is addressed to owners of private small to medium-sized companies who compose the backbone of the domestic economy. We wrote this book to provide you with good nuts and bolts advice on how to go about selling your business. The book addresses all of the fundamental questions and challenges involved in putting together a deal for your company. We also recommend this book to accountants, lawyers, business consultants and even potential buyers, so that they too can have a better understanding of how the process works and how deals get done.

Selling is one of the most important decisions you will ever make regarding your company. It is also one of the most important personal economic decisions you will face. And yet, all too often, owners of private companies will enter into negotiations without any proper planning, totally unprepared for the many complex issues involved in selling.

As is true with most things in life, planning pays. Selling a business should warrant at least as much planning and preparation as any other major corporate undertaking, such as a plant expansion or a new product introduction. You need to give this project the time, effort and attention that it deserves.

All too often, private business owners view selling in a negative light; they consider selling only when in dire trouble. In this book, we attempt to dispel this specious notion. As you accumulate earnings in your business, it is essential that you periodically evaluate the option of selling to reclaim those assets. In addition, selling can help you to better position your company for growth by feeding off of the capital and capabilities of a larger parent. Rather than a negative move, selling can truly be a liberating step for both you and your company.

The main point that we stress throughout this book is that selling requires selling. In the end, selling your company is no different than selling any other product: you need to plan your strategy, position your product, and then aggressively take action. If you take a cavalier attitude and ignore your customer (in this case, the buyer), then you will most probably fail – like all other companies that refuse to respond to their customers.

This book should serve as a guide to steer you through each phase of the selling process, providing the techniques necessary to negotiate a good deal while highlighting the common mistakes and problems to avoid. The format of this book follows the basic sequence of the selling process, from planning a strategy and establishing a value, to structuring a deal and negotiating the agreements.

Mergers and acquisitions are, by their very nature, very technical creatures, involving many complex legal, accounting and tax issues. We have attempted to make this book as user-friendly and accessible as possible, though at times we need to digress into technical areas. You need not retain all of the financial or legal meanderings to get a grasp of the process and what it entails.

Given the complexity of the various matters related to acquisitions, it is important to realize that this book cannot possibly take the place of your accountant or legal adviser in providing expert advice on your specific situation. This book is meant only to introduce general concepts and provide an overview of the process. Selling your business is too important a matter not to get the best advice you can.

There are no domestic markets today; all markets have become international. This is especially true of mergers and acquisitions, where it has become just as likely that the ultimate buyer of your company will come from across a national border as across town. While our merger advisory business is based in New York and our orientation is to the American markets, the content of this book is global in nature. Our client base of sellers and the universe of buyers has become as international as the markets. While there are a few different 'wrinkles' depending on culture or legal systems, the basic message of this book is as relevant to a business owner in Los Angeles as in Liverpool.

We provide many examples in this book, some based on actual clients, some based on composites. We appreciate those former clients who allowed us to profile their situations in order to emphasize salient points.

Certain people have been very generous with their time and efforts in helping us put this book together. Special thanks should go to Cynthia Lam who toiled long and hard in helping us to research and write the manuscript. Jim Abbott of Carter, Ledyard & Milburn deserves recognition for casting a watchful eye over the various sections relating to the legal and tax aspects of a deal. We also tip our hat to David Mitchell for introducing us to Spencer Smith at Kogan Page, who has been very understanding and accommodating throughout this process.

Lastly, we owe gratitude to the hundreds of business owners we have talked to or worked with over the years. It is through our experience with these owners that we were able to write this book. In essence, they are really the authors.

ONE

Why Sell?

Private business owners decide to sell their companies for a variety of reasons. Though each owner probably considers his circumstances to be unique, most actually share similar concerns and motivations. In this chapter, we highlight many of the common reasons why owners consider selling. We also explain how you can determine the ideal time to sell in order to achieve the most advantageous deal.

REASONS FOR SELLING

If you are like most business owners, you will probably consider selling your company for one of, or a combination of, the five following reasons:

1. *Retirement:* you want to retire or to reduce the amount of time you spend working in your business.

2. *Succession:* there exists no family member or logical second-tier manager to take over your company.

3. *Diversity of assets:* as most of your net worth is tied up in your company, you want to diversify your assets, as well as gain some liquidity.

4. *Capital for growth:* you see a need for additional external capital to continue to grow your company.

5. *Association with a larger firm:* you seek the broader distribution channels, marketing strengths or manufacturing efficiencies that a larger firm can offer.

1. Retirement or a reduction of time spent in the business

You probably believe that you work far harder than your friends or acquaintances who do not own their own companies. In most cases, you are right. Indeed, it is precisely your commitment and devotion to your business that enabled it to flourish in the first place. Many owners believe that if they are not the first one to arrive in the morning and the last to leave at night, their businesses will suffer. While maintaining a frantic pace of life may be challenging, stimulating and fun (and, indeed, necessary in building a business), at some point most owners decide that they want to slow down.

A few years ago, we represented Robert Schmalzried, the owner of Dunham's, a large chain of discount sporting goods stores located in the American Midwest. After a life-long career working for major retailers, Bob Schmalzried decided to establish his own business in his early 60s. In just five years, he built a business generating over $70 million of revenues from ten retail locations. While he had assembled an excellent management team, Bob Schmalzried remained the driving force behind the company.

A tall and commanding man, Bob was well regarded in the sporting goods community as a keen competitor and an excellent merchant. He still travelled regularly to New York to oversee the buying for the company.

When we first met him, Bob told us that he would never have considered selling if he were ten years younger. He saw unlimited opportunities for his new retailing concept and believed that Dunham's was on the verge of exploding growth. However, having toiled through the start-up phase of the company, Bob just did not have the spark to continue at the same pace to grow it. He eventually decided that his only alternative was to sell the business.

After considering numerous offers for his company, Bob Schmalzried decided to sell Dunham's to a large NYSE-listed retailing firm. While there were several reasons he preferred his eventual buyer over others, the major consideration was the fact that the acquirer had a strong and deep management team in the speciality retailing area. Immediately after the sale was completed, the buyer transferred one of their senior retailing executives to Dunham's to assume the management of the company. Bob Schmalzried did not immediately retire, but the sale did enable him to scale back his time and involvement in the day-to-day operations. The result was that Bob could remain active in the business, without the on-going responsibilities or headaches of running the business.

Once a sole owner of a company decides to retire or reduce his time in a business, a sale of the company is the natural path to take. However, a sale is also a logical alternative when only one of many partners decides to retire and the others cannot or do not want to assume the burden of buying out the retiring partner. Quite often, partners who want to continue with the business cannot possibly afford to buy out a departing partner at fair market value. Even if those remaining could afford the buyout, they are often reluctant to shoulder the entire responsibility of running the company, especially if they are incurring significant debt to buy out the departing partner. In such instances, a sale of the company can not only provide liquidity to all partners but can also be structured in a way that provides on-going jobs, equity participation and incentives to the remaining partners.

2. Succession concerns

One of the most common problems all owners face is the question of who will succeed them when they retire or are forced to leave because of illness. Most owners are undoubtedly the inspiration and main driving force behind their companies. As such, they find it difficult to delegate responsibility to others. Even when owners can delegate responsibility, most small businesses simply do not need layers of senior management, nor can they support the overhead. Undoubtedly, you are tremendously important to the success of your business. Should anything serious happen to you, your company would suffer dramatically from lack of direction and stability.

Recently, we were exposed to an extreme example of a succession problem. We had been in touch with an owner of a manufacturing concern for many years. While he appeared interested in selling, he never had the time to focus his attention on the matter. This owner was in his early 60s and apparently in good health; the issue of selling never seemed especially pressing to him.

After many months of no contact, the owner's son eventually called us. Unfortunately, his father had suddenly dropped dead of a heart attack, leaving the company with no senior management in place. The son had been forced to quit his job, uproot his family to move back to his home town, and take over the running of the company, for which he was ill-prepared. The son had grown up in the business, but he had never actually assumed any management role. Naturally, the son was anxious to sell the company as quickly as possible, at a significantly reduced value. Needless to say, a more farsighted succession plan would have prevented such a difficult situation. By not planning better, the owner both unsettled his son's life and greatly diminished the value of the business (and thus the estate for his wife).

Many small business owners equate success with the creation of a family dynasty. They founded their companies to be 'family businesses', to be passed down from one generation to the next, providing both a familial bond and economic prosperity. Yet, reality displays quite a different picture. Studies by both the US Small Business Administration and Wharton School at the University of Pennsylvania show that only about 25 per cent of private businesses are passed from one generation to the next, and less than one in ten make it to a third generation. Regardless of a founder's grand plans, he must eventually face the fact that, more often than not, his business will not be passed on to the next generation.

Most children have neither an interest in, nor a proclivity for, the family business. Just as likely, an owner's children are not the most capable candidates to take over the reins of his company. If an owner has two children who work for the family business and one child is clearly the more competent, promoting one over the other may cause severe problems. Similarly, there may be a competent non-family member who should rightfully succeed the owner as President, even though a son may argue that it is his birthright to succeed to the President's job. In all of these cases, selling may provide a rational and fair solution for succession issues.

We recently represented a company that was owned by two brothers, aged 38 and 43, and their 55-year old uncle. The two brothers were effectively running the company; their uncle had significantly reduced both his responsibilities and the time he spent in the business. The uncle owned one-half of the company's stock; the two brothers each owned 25 per cent. The uncle was interested in selling his stock and, within a short period of time, retiring.

The easy and logical solution would have been for the two nephews to buy out their uncle's share. The company had an available line of credit that could be used to finance such an acquisition. On-going management was not an issue, as the two brothers could clearly run the company without their uncle. When we put this proposal to the family, there was an uncomfortable pause in the conversation. Later, the uncle took us aside and explained the situation. The younger brother was, in fact, much the stronger of the two. While the two brothers got along quite well, the older brother refused to participate in an acquisition if he could not be in charge. The older brother just could not bring himself to take a junior position to his younger brother. Hence, the three decided to sell the entire company to an outside party.

Establishing a protégé or a strong second tier of management obviously helps to address succession problems. However, in reality, this 'sharing of power' is often difficult to effect. Recently, we worked with a leading manufacturer of consumer items. The company was owned by two very able brothers, whose father had started the firm 50 years earlier. After 40 years in the business themselves, the brothers decided they wanted to scale back their direct involvement. A decision was made to search for a management team of experienced industry people to run their company. After a thorough search, they hired several executives, all of whom had impressive backgrounds working for larger companies.

The brothers immediately began to work part-time, allowing the new team to take over the reins of the business. They initially vowed to yield full financial and operating responsibility to the new managers; yet, over time, the brothers began to question or review every decision. All significant policy changes were resisted.

Six months after bringing in the new team, the brothers found themselves worrying about the business as much, if not more, than when they actually ran the company. After all, they still owned the company's equity and still remained the ones most directly affected by bad business decisions. Thus, it almost came as a relief when management's decision to diversify into a new market failed. After four quarters of deteriorating earnings, the brothers fired or demoted all of their new managers and resumed running the company.

After their failed experience with 'professional' managers, the brothers decided that the only acceptable path to retirement would be a complete sale to outsiders. By selling, the brothers would be transferring the search for the 'right' management team and the equity risk of that decision to the buyer.

Owners are often faced with situations where they have built their companies to a certain level of sales and market share, only to feel that they require managers with greater experience or different talents to take their companies to the next plateau.

Two owners of a UK-based medical products company recently provided a specific example of this. The two founders started their company after long careers with a large medical products company. The one owner's forte was marketing; the other provided the engineering talent. In five years, their company grew to over £20 million in annual revenues. Both were proud of their accomplishments and clearly capable of guiding a profitable, growing company. However, both also felt unsettled with their new roles as executive officers of a quickly growing company. Each felt more comfortable and capable in their respective areas of marketing and engineering. So, they sought to sell their company to a party that would assume the strategic planning and operating responsibilities, while allowing both men the chance to concentrate instead on their strengths.

3. Diversification of assets

Perhaps the most common reason for owners to consider selling their companies is the desire to increase their liquidity and diversify their assets. Private companies are generally very illiquid investments; no ready markets provide for a quick sale of part or all of a private company. Generally, earnings must be ploughed back into a company for increased receivables or inventory, or to purchase additional equipment. Thus, most of a private company's 'return' is actually reinvested back into an already illiquid investment.

Similarly, with most of your net worth retained in your business, you constantly risk your financial position with each major business decision or market development. A major plant expansion or new product development always brings with it new or greater risk. With all of your proverbial eggs in one basket, you may eventually tire of constantly risking your financial security on your company's continued prosperity.

Most private companies are founded on relatively small amounts of capital. Thus, early on, a business owner risks very little except his time and effort in building his business. In the early years of any business's evolution, growth almost demands risk. Because start-ups are worth relatively little, owners are generally quite willing to place their businesses on the line to achieve growth. Yet, as businesses mature, generate significant capital bases and evolve into major assets, many owners become more and more reticent to continually risk their companies with each major new strategic move.

Selling your business allows you to bring some liquidity and diversification to your holdings, and to more rationally disperse your net worth among many asset classes. You can lessen your dependence on the continued success of your company and, at the same time, be in a position to enjoy your wealth.

We recently worked with the owners of a precision aluminium casting operation. The company was extremely profitable; however, the three owners felt obliged to continually reinvest all of their earnings in new plant and equipment to remain competitive. While the three received salaries commensurate with their jobs, they did not have much disposable wealth. Their personal net worths were impressive, on paper. None felt particularly wealthy, however, as all of their net worth was tied up in the company. Should their business fortunes reverse, they feared, most of their wealth would disappear.

A sale allowed the owners to make their holdings 'liquid' and to realize a return on their years of effort. All three owners stayed on in their same capacities and continued to run the company as before. However, their personal bank accounts were such that should anything ever happen to the company, they could retire quite comfortably and never work again.

This example is far from an anomaly; in our experience, most owners *do* stay on to run their companies after they have been sold. Many subsequently believe that they are actually better managers after a sale than when they owned their companies. No longer do they feel that they are putting their companies (and thus their net worths) on the line each time they make a new strategic decision. Consequently, they feel free to take the prudent and appropriate risks that they might not have otherwise made had they continued to own their companies.

4. Expansion capital

Companies may require additional capital. If they are growing quickly, owners may find that their cash demands outpace their resources. It is not uncommon for a quickly growing company to suddenly fall due to its own weight because it could not meet its growing cash needs. By definition, growth means increased receivables and inventory. In addition, an expanding business requires continued investment in plant, equipment, training, advertising, distribution and an administrative and sales staff. Many small companies do not generate enough earnings internally to keep up with growing capital demands. Banks, the traditional source of funding for small companies, are generally reluctant to lend enough capital to maintain aggressive growth rates. Banks are constrained by formal ratios and lending covenants, which necessarily focus more on downside conservatism than growth possibilities.

Our prior examination of the Dunham's chain provides an interesting example of a growing company's capital needs outstripping its internal capabilities. When the company was sold, it operated ten stores, all in the American Midwest. Through internally generated cash and bank borrowings, the company had the financial resources available to open approximately three stores a year. However, in the fiercely competitive business of speciality retailing, Dunham's management knew that they needed to move quickly to establish themselves. Theirs was a unique marketing concept, but one that could be easily replicated by another company if they did not take the initiative to grow rapidly and establish a 'critical mass'.

The owner, Bob Schmalzried, quickly determined that only with an injection of outside money could he properly capitalize on the market opportunities. His sale of the company helped him to realize his goal; in the three years subsequent to the sale, Dunham's grew from ten stores to over 60, with a large share of each regional market in which they operate. It would have taken over a decade for the company to have achieved that growth through internally-generated cash, if they could have achieved it at all.

5. Association with a larger company

Acquirers can bring more to private companies than just capital. Larger, more diverse companies can bring intangible advantages such as: wider and more developed sales and distribution channels; a larger, more sophisticated advertising and marketing capability; manufacturing and administrative efficiencies; and engineering and technical support. While these intangible advantages are rarely the main motivation for an owner to sell, they often become quite important once they are discovered.

One of our clients, a manufacturer of processing equipment for the petroleum industry, found that revenues could double in one year by switching from the company's manufacturer's representatives to the acquirer's direct marketing channels. Likewise, a recent client in the tyre distribution business found that administrative costs such as insurance and workers' benefits dropped by 50 per cent after the firm was acquired.

TIMING

One last factor you should consider prior to deciding to sell is the timing of a sale. Timing is a subject not often addressed or discussed by owners, but it is perhaps one of the most important factors in terms of successfully selling a business.

Like the stock and property markets, the markets for private companies rise and fall. It is important to be cognisant of the relative strengths of the markets in setting goals for a sale of a business. Clearly, by timing a sale to coincide with a strong market, you improve your chances of achieving your price and other objectives. There are three major elements to consider in the timing of a sale: 1) the macro or general economic environment; 2) the outlook of your company's industry; and 3) the relative prospects and performance of your company in particular.

Like biorhythms, the ideal time to consider a sale is when the prospects of all three are rising and the outlook remains healthy. Yet, as in biorhythms, it is rather rare that one can find a perfect time when all three indicators are just about to reach their apex. Thus, timing becomes more of an art than a science, anticipating which of the three factors will matter most to potential acquirers in the marketplace.

Buyers' psychology, not unlike consumers' psychology, is subject to general perceptions of the state of the world. Just as the stock market will often rise or fall depending on world affairs, interest from potential acquirers is often dependent on external matters and events.

Turning first to the general economic matters, it is obvious that one of the best times to consider selling is when the economy is experiencing sustained growth, low unemployment, a good trade balance and a rising stock market. Indeed, over the past five decades, there has been a high correlation between general economic growth and merger and acquisition activity. Times of generally stable growth and low interest rates correspond favourably to healthy acquisition markets and, thus, healthy pricing. Times of a stagnant economy or rising interest rates have lowered demand for acquisitions and resulted in lower overall values.

During most of the 1970s, the world economies were generally stagnant, interest rates were running at double-digit rates, unemployment was high, and most of the international stock markets were depressed. Large corporations were, in general, unenthusiastic about buying companies – most were more concerned about stabilizing their own businesses than growing or diversifying through acquisitions. Thus, the 1970s were a period of weak demand for companies, resulting in a stagnant acquisition market and depressed values. Many very healthy and successful firms generated tepid interest and weak pricing. Those that could often chose to delay selling their business.

The 1980s presented a much different picture: interest rates were as low as half what they had been in the 1970s, stock markets rebounded dramatically, and the world's GNP again grew at a strong rate. All of these positive economic indicators generated optimistic perceptions as to the market. Optimism increased demand: merger activity involving private companies doubled from 1979 to 1989. Correspondingly, the average price/earnings ratio paid for acquisition targets doubled in the same period. Many companies that would have attracted only low levels of interest in the 1970s were suddenly in the enviable position of having several good offers from which to choose.

The 1990s have been a decade of contrasts. The early part of the decade suffered from a worldwide recession and a hangover caused by over-leverage in the financial markets. The result was a soft merger and acquisition market, and a corresponding dip in relative prices. By mid-decade, however, as the world's economies started to grow once again, and corporations began to focus on the internationalization of markets, merger and acquisition activity began to blossom. Rising stock prices and a huge availability of equity and debt money drove activity and pricing to record levels.

The same general market perceptions that apply to macro factors also apply to the overall health of a company's industry. When an industry is growing and shows signs of continued prosperity, it reflects well on all companies in that industry. Unfortunately, the converse is also true. A receding tide lowers all boats, and a splendid company within a sick industry will be running against the tide in convincing potential acquirers of its desirability. Of course, if an industry is notoriously cyclical, such as housing or capital equipment, an owner should consider selling while the industry is expanding. Once the contraction begins, he may have to wait through another turn of the cycle to generate significant interest in his business.

Returning to the Dunham's example for a moment, Bob Schmalzried took advantage of growing interest in the speciality retailing field to determine the appropriate time to market his company. Many large public retailers were trading at high multiples and viewed speciality retailing as a high-growth area for diversification. By timing his sale to coincide with strong market interest, Bob Schmalzried was able to maximize the eventual price for his business.

Another example was the owner of a company that produced drill bits for the oil industry. In the early 1980s, after a considerable run-up in oil prices, he decided to sell his company. All the major oil companies were very keen on locking up a source of supply for bits, because replacement parts had become hard to source. After playing many competing suitors against one another, the company was sold for a very high price to an industry buyer.

One year after the sale, the seller's friend decided that he, too, wanted to sell his company, which provided services to the off-shore oil industry. The catalyst for the sale was the great deal he saw our client get for his company. However, just as the owner of the service company decided to sell, the bottom fell out of the oil market. Drilling for oil dried up. Though the company had a number of attractive contracts and continued to prosper in the early years of the oil downturn, the market ignored his company completely, primarily because it was in what was perceived as an unattractive industry. After a year of marketing the company, we could find no buyers, even at a very low price. We finally advised our client to wait until the oil business rebounded before once again considering a sale.

The last and most vital factor to consider in weighing the timing of a sale is the specific performance and prospects of the company being sold. The ideal time to consider selling is when current performance is good, and prospects appear even better. Just as banks are most eager to lend money when a company has no immediate need for it, acquirers tend to be most interested in companies that are not under the gun to sell and that have no clouds on the horizon. It is safe to assume that most buyers are at least as prescient and intuitive as sellers. Buyers can generally ascertain when a business's fortunes are about to turn downward.

When you sell a company that still appears to have plenty of opportunity and momentum, you can sell positive future prospects and therefore command a generous price. If questions exist as to future growth or profitability, or a downturn or loss is inevitable, acquirers will tend to focus on the short-term problems to the exclusion of the past performance or other inherent merits of the business.

A steady track record of profitability and growth will help to convince an acquirer that the trend will continue. From a value point of view, it is often quite advantageous for you to take the time to address and fix problems rather than accept the inevitable discounts you will face in selling a business with an uncertain future. Indeed, it is a fact of the marketplace that acquirers often overpay for well-run businesses promising good growth and severely discount poorly performing companies.

One of the most serious errors you can make is trying to squeeze the last pound out of your growth trend, leaving nothing to the potential acquirers. To pay a high price, acquirers have to believe that they are buying into a flourishing business. Markets and business conditions change too dramatically for you ever to be able to time a sale at the exact 'top' of the curve.

For most companies, the opportunity to clinch a great deal is a fleeting one; you must be prepared to act when all the signals are right. For that reason, even if a sale of the business is not an immediate goal, you should still periodically examine your business and its prospects in the market. This exercise will show you how the market might view and value your business. It will also allow you to better understand the dynamics of how changes in the market or in your business performance will influence the relative attractiveness of your company and its value.

A Sale Versus a Public Offering

You will eventually reach a point where you must make a vital decision regarding the future of your business. Should you hold onto your highly illiquid and risky investment and expand your company alone, reaping all the benefits for yourself? Or, alternatively, should you take steps to increase your liquidity and lessen your risks, giving up some future profits in the process?

This dilemma often propels a private company owner down one of two paths: an initial public offering (IPO) or a sale. In this chapter, we will examine these two options and discuss the differing solutions they provide regarding risk, liquidity and growth.

Simply put, an IPO turns a private company into a public one. In an IPO, a private company, or its shareholders, sell a certain percentage of the company's stock to the public. In return for these shares, the company or its shareholders receive cash. An owner taking his business public has the choice as to how much he will be diluted in terms of ownership. Most owners are interested in maintaining their control positions and choose to sell only a minority of their stock. Typically, an underwriter, or a firm hired to act as agent in placing the shares with the public, is retained to handle the offering.

Once your business goes public, you will immediately discover many changes beyond simply the increase in the number of your shareholders. After an IPO, a newly public company must conform with the relevant government, financial and legal requirements. Among other things, securities regulators require all public companies to file quarterly reports on their performance and operations, which become publicly available information. It is through these quarterly reports that the company communicates with its shareholders and other potential investors.

As an owner of a private company used to disclosing nothing about your business to outsiders, such public reporting will seem disconcerting at first. Competitors and customers alike can access such detailed information as operating margins and labour costs. Most CEOs of newly public companies are not prepared for the sudden public availability of their previously private operating data (including your compensation, which can be obtained through the annual proxy statement). Many owners compare running a public company to 'living in a fishbowl'.

Even more disturbing to former owners of private businesses is the on-going cost of being a public company. Between legal, auditing, investment banking, public relations, printing and mailing costs, the annual expense for being a public company starts at $250 000 (£150 000) and rises quickly.

For many, if not most, private companies, a public offering is not a viable option. Compared to the millions of small to medium-sized private companies in the US, there are fewer than 10 000 publicly listed firms on the New York Stock Exchange, American Stock Exchange and NASDAQ National Market Listing (including such names as DuPont, Merck and General Motors). In England, the universe is ever smaller; the London Stock Exchange boasts under 2500 listed names, of which, over 500 are foreign firms. In Canada, the totals for both the Toronto and Vancouver Exchanges are less than 3000.

Clearly, the vast majority of private companies are not candidates to 'go public'. For owners facing retirement or succession dilemmas, an IPO is clearly not a viable alternative. Many private companies just do not have sufficient 'critical mass' or are not the types of businesses that would command interest in the public markets. Yet, for those whose companies have the appropriate characteristics, an IPO can offer tremendous advantages. The most significant advantage is the opportunity to achieve some liquidity for yourself and to raise capital for your business, all without yielding control of your company.

Owners considering a sale need to weigh the relative strengths and weaknesses of an IPO before determining which path to take. Only by seriously considering an IPO can you be certain that the decision to sell is best for you.

Both an IPO and a sale offer significantly different realities for owners of private companies, specifically in the areas of:

- the amount and extent of liquidity you achieve;
- the growth possibilities afforded your company;
- your continued control over operations and strategic planning;
- the stability of the respective markets.

LIQUIDITY

A sale of a business obviously provides you with the most natural path to liquidity. Through a sale, you are able to reclaim your assets from your company and spread them among numerous other, more liquid investments. A sale also eliminates all on-going business risk. Whether you stay on to run the business or not, a sale frees you from the financial concerns of the business. No longer does your net worth rise and fall with the fortunes of your company.

Though some sale transactions involve either a retention of some equity in your business or other on-going contingent payments, a sale typically leaves you with only minor participation in the future growth or success of your company. Whatever 'upside' gains that are generated in the future belong to the acquirer.

An IPO, on the other hand, allows you to actively participate in the continued 'upside' of the business. Through an IPO, you retain significant equity in the future growth of the company. (Of course, the converse is also true: you also share significantly in the 'downside' risk.)

While an IPO provides immediate cash to the business and to you personally, you will continue to hold much of your wealth in company stock, the liquidity and value of which is exposed to business (and stock market) vagaries.

Generally, most companies with market capitalizations of less than $50 million (£30 million) find that their stock has little aftermarket float (in other words, it is not traded often enough or in large enough quantity to allow one to sell or buy without dramatically disrupting price). Even for companies with market values of over $50 million, the possibility always exists that sufficient secondary markets do not develop for their stock, making it difficult for investors to trade their shares. Investors tend to seek those stocks that offer a sense of order and fluidity in trading patterns. For a public company with little float on its stock, it is quite possible for an owner to have no more liquidity than when he was private.

To provide continued access to capital for both a company and its shareholders through subsequent stock offerings, the CEO of a public company must work to ensure that a deep and dependable market exists for his company's shares. The traditional solution to this problem is to go public using an underwriter with the size, clout and commitment to follow the stock after the initial offering. The larger, more-established underwriters like Merrill Lynch and Goldman Sachs have stock analysts to follow and research their client's shares, and stock brokers to stir up interest in their stocks. These larger underwriters act as diligent 'market makers' and provide active aftermarket support.

Yet, it is not easy to attract a good underwriter's attention. In the US alone, significantly less than half of all public companies attract major brokerage houses to either maintain research or make markets in their stocks.

GROWTH POSSIBILITIES

An IPO generates immediate capital to fund your company's growth plans. Often, the greater a company's growth opportunities, the greater its capital needs. If a public company requires continued funding to exploit new growth opportunities, it will have to return to the public markets to raise additional money. As discussed earlier, subsequent public offerings are conditional on the performance of the company and the market for the stock.

A sale on the other hand can provide continued access to capital through its parent. In addition, a sale can provide greater resources than merely the acquirer's capital. A larger company with the 'right' fit can bring manufacturing and production efficiencies, wider distribution channels, broader marketing capabilities, a share of the administrative and overhead burden, and a greater general stature in the market. The ice-cream maker Haagen-Dazs established an international presence and distribution far quicker and more efficiently under the aegis of Pillsbury than would have been possible had it remained independent. By selling to the 'right' party, a company can position itself to take advantage of its acquirer's strengths to grow at an even quicker pace than it had on its own.

CONTROL

The retention of control is probably the single greatest advantage of an IPO. Most owners going through an IPO emerge in control of their companies. It is this very feature that prompts many business owners to seek an IPO.

In a sale, even if you remain as CEO of the company, you will ultimately lose total command over your company. Regardless of promises made by an acquirer or the operating duties retained after a sale, once your business has been sold you transfer ultimate authority to the acquirer. This can be a difficult fact for some owners to accept, especially those remaining in an executive capacity. Rightly or wrongly, no new owner will operate your company exactly as you have. This, of course, can be cause for either resentment or arguments.

While owners who take their businesses public do generally maintain control, they are still answerable to their public shareholders and the market at large. Most private business owners are not accustomed to operating to the City's short-term standards, being judged solely by quarterly results.

Indeed, the performance of the stock in the aftermarket is the yardstick by which every public company (and its management) is ultimately measured. Not coincidentally, the performance of the stock also becomes the yardstick by which the CEO's net worth is measured. While a CEO may 'control' his public company, his fortunes are still subject to the vagaries of the market.

STABILITY OF THE MARKETS

There is quite a contrast between the relative stability of the IPO market and the acquisition market. In general, the IPO market is significantly more volatile. Over the past two decades, it has not been uncommon for the number of public offerings to jump dramatically from one year to next. Both individual and institutional appetite for IPOs changes rapidly, depending on overall stock market conditions and the liquidity in financial markets. Regardless of your own company's performance and prospects, when the IPO window is closed, it is almost impossible to raise money in the markets.

In the US, the total number of IPOs jumped over 500 per cent from 1982 to 1983, and then fell by almost 50 per cent the next year. Likewise, IPO activity dropped 30 per cent from 1993 to 1995, only to gain 52 per cent in 1996 and fall again by 28 per cent in 1997.

While the merger and acquisition markets have displayed some ebb and flow of activity over the past two decades, the general trend has been more consistent and stable. Indeed, while international merger activity at the end of 1998 was over four times greater than in 1980, the trend has been marked by steady year-on-year growth, not violent swings from one peak to a new valley.

Both the IPO and M&A markets are closely tied to the general business and financial markets. However, the IPO market has a far greater tendency to open wide for certain opportunities, only to close abruptly. During periods of peak activity and interest, the IPO market tends to offer higher overall company valuations and greater receptivity to marginal deals. However, it is important for owners to move quickly when the IPO markets are hot, as history has demonstrated that periods of high demand are often quickly followed by periods of great malaise.

The merger market, on the other hand, is more consistent and predictable. Activity and pricing does move up and down with the overall markets, but within relatively narrow bands. The merger market is always open and receptive to good deals, unlike the IPO market. Large strategic buyers are always seeking growth, geographic expansion and new products through acquisitions.

An owner considering going public must keep an eye on the relative strength of the IPO markets in judging the timing of his move. Though the health of the markets is an important consideration in a sale, it is certainly a less crucial factor than in an IPO.

THREE

What Your Company is Worth: A Question of Value

Just as beauty is in the eye of the beholder, a company's value is determined by the interest it generates in the market. You may believe that your company is worth $30 million (£20 million), but if the best offer you can get from the market is $15 million (£10 million), then your company is only worth $15 million (£10 million).

While there are numerous quantitative methods you can employ to estimate the value of your business, the true value can only be determined by the market. By definition, fair market value is the price that a commodity can bring in an open exchange between knowledgeable buyers and sellers in an unfettered market. Valuations are done in the abstract; transactions in the concrete.

Unless the person preparing the valuation of your company subsequently makes you an offer, the valuation may prove to be meaningless. No valuation study, however exhaustive or detailed, can determine the actual market value of your company. Only buyers can do that. Regardless of the conclusions of any independent analysis and valuation, it takes two parties, a buyer and a seller, to agree on a price, complete a transaction and set a true value on your company.

A company whose securities trade in a public forum benefits from having its value set on a daily basis. Private companies are not so fortunate. There is probably nothing more difficult in finance than placing a value on a company for which no market exists.

By its very nature, a valuation is an estimate of the price that a company could bring in the open market. At its best, a valuation can give you some idea of what range of prices you might expect to realize in the market. However, you need to recognize a valuation for what it is: merely one opinion of the ultimate worth of your business. Valuations are more art than science, and a very imprecise art at that.

A few years ago, we were engaged to sell a California-based distributor of industrial products. After dutiful quantitative analysis, we concluded that the client's business was worth approximately $12–

14 million. After soliciting bids from a number of logical suitors, we were quite dismayed when all of the offers came in around $10 million.

We searched further and were able to locate a large British manufacturer of engineered parts that was interested in expanding its distribution to the west coast of America. To our astonishment, the British firm came in with an initial offer of $16 million (£9.6 million). Obviously, the British rationalized their offer by how well our client fitted in with their own strategic plans. It was clearly cheaper to acquire our client than to incur the cost of starting their own operation and suffering through several years of losses. The acquisition would also have the additional benefit of eliminating one of their potential competitors. We were eventually able to negotiate the British company up to $17 million (£10.2 million), a deal that is still talked about in the industry today.

Just as our valuation model overestimated the offers we expected to generate from the domestic bidders, it significantly underestimated the value the British group saw in the business. There was no way to justify this differential using common valuation techniques. The British were not employing our valuation methods; they obviously viewed this deal from quite a different perspective.

Before going to market, you should first go through the process of estimating a range of potential values for your business. Even assuming their inherent limitations, valuation studies can none the less provide you with some general indications as to what prices might be both realistic and realizable. It is always advisable to have a complete and detailed understanding of possible values at the outset, so selling shareholders and advisers alike are clear as to expectations and realistic goals.

(In understanding the concepts presented in this chapter, it is important to recognize that value is being defined in terms of cash or cash equivalents. It is clear that £10 million in cash value is not equal to £10 million in a 4 per cent, 20-year, unsecured note. In describing various methods of estimating a company's value, we are generally talking about its cash value, or 'present value' in merger parlance.)

Over the years, certain methods of valuation have come to be accepted by professionals in the merger industry. While literally dozens of different quantitative approaches have been developed, you should only focus on those methods that are commonly employed by buyers and lenders in the market. After all, by using the same methods, you and your suitors will at least be approaching the question of value from the same perspective. You may not agree with buyers on either their assumptions or their conclusions, but at least you can negotiate and argue from a common ground.

There is no single factor on which value hinges. Value is ultimately determined by a combination of numerous elements, including a company's assets, its past performance, its future earnings prospects, the outlook of its industry and geographic market, and the strength of such intangibles as management and products.

Each potential acquirer will look at your company from a different vantage point, with differing motivations as to why they want to buy your company. Some suitors may be seeking to broaden their markets; others may be looking to bring manufacturing capabilities in-house. Still others may simply be looking for new opportunities in which to invest their cash.

Every acquirer will have their own, internal methods of valuing your business. Depending on such factors as their cost of money, potential operating synergies or alternative opportunities, each acquirer will develop their own, unique perspective on the value of your company.

APPROACHES TO VALUATION

Three fundamental approaches to valuation have come to be commonly accepted in the merger field:

1.   the asset approach;

2.   the market comparison approach;

3.   the income capitalization approach.

Although these methods vary in their applicability, depending on specific facts or circumstances, they do at least indicate a range of values based on certain commonly accepted fundamentals and principles. By analysing the values indicated by each of these three methods, coupled with an understanding of current market conditions, you can form an objective opinion as to the fair value of your company. The three basic approaches to valuation are defined below.

1. Asset approach

In the asset approach, the underlying tangible assets of an enterprise are considered individually. The sum of the fair values of each asset, after netting out the aggregate total of the company's tangible liabilities, represents the asset value of a company.

There are a number of different derivations of asset-based valuations; they can be based on either liquidation value, replacement cost value or fair market value. Of these, fair market value is generally considered the most appropriate.

'Book value' (or the carrying value of assets minus the stated liabilities) should not be a consideration. Book value is not really a definition of value, but rather an accounting concept fraught with the vagaries of differing depreciation methods and accounting policies. Book value represents the historic cost of a company's assets, not their market values. It can easily be adjusted to market value, however, by considering such obvious factors as excess depreciation, LIFO reserves, inventory 'cushions' and unstated assets, as well as updated appraisals of fixed assets.

The asset approach is generally considered most appropriate for companies with significant tangible assets, such as real estate holding companies or natural resource companies. Asset-based valuations are also germane for those companies that do not generate an acceptable return on their assets. Such companies are often worth more dead than alive, and are usually sold for their asset values prior to being liquidated.

Owners of profitable companies generally assume that asset-based valuations are not suitable for their situations. These owners tend to believe that their companies should be valued on their profitability, market presence and other intangible benefits, not merely the worth of their tangible assets. There is certainly some logic to this argument. Most valuation studies do indeed emphasize the profitability (or anticipated profitability) of the subject companies.

No valuation, however, can ignore the question of a company's underlying assets. Value is always based on an interplay between a company's assets and its profits. While profits (or potential profits) may be the more salient factor in determining value, buyers tend to scorn 'paying up' for a deal that involves too few assets and too much goodwill. Thus, each buyer will examine your asset base in great detail before determining an acceptable value. Everything else being equal, a company that can deliver a higher asset value is worth more, primarily because the transaction generates less goodwill for the buyer. ('Goodwill' is explained in greater detail in Chapter 7.)

2. Market comparison approach

The market comparison approach compares your company's operations and financial performance with that of 1) similar publicly traded companies and 2) recent sale transactions involving like private companies. Since you are estimating the value of your company for acquisition purposes, the merger markets will generally provide a more accurate benchmark than a comparison with publicly traded companies.

The market comparison approach is similar to the methodology used in the property market. By looking at transactions involving other like properties, you can generate a good understanding of the range of values in which your property should trade.

A full comparative analysis examines such factors as: price/earnings ratios, price/book value ratios, price/sales ratios, debt-to-equity ratios, return on sales (profits/sales), return on assets (profits/assets), and return on equity (profits/shareholders' equity). Of these, the most broadly used comparative measure is the price/earnings (P/E) ratio. For private companies, this ratio generally represents the indicated price (or value) over the current operating profit (before taxes and interest), and is expressed as a multiple of earnings. P/E multiples are used to gauge broad investor sentiment toward the economy in general and your industry and company in particular. Companies that offer above-average growth possibilities tend to command higher P/E multiples. Conversely, companies that operate in mundane industries or offer little in the way of growth opportunities generally trade at low P/Es.

If a comparative analysis finds that companies broadly similar to yours tend to sell for 5-7 times current operating earnings, then you might safely assume that acquirers would expect to pay the same for your company. If, however, your company operates at a 40 per cent gross margin versus the industry average of 30 per cent, then you may well be able to justify a premium to the comparative industry average, based on your superior operating capabilities. By comparing your operating ratios with the comparative 'peer' group, you will be able to make a subjective determination of where in the range of pricing ratios your company should trade.

A P/E multiple can also be expressed in its inverse form, called the capitalization rate (a multiple of 5 corresponds to a 20 per cent capitalization rate). The capitalization rate represents an annualized return an investor should expect (or demand) from his investment.

US Treasury Notes or other sovereign governmental obligations are defined by the market as being 'riskless' investments. If Treasuries are yielding 6–7 per cent, most investors or acquirers will demand a premium over that return to be 'induced' to make another, riskier investment. Because most smaller, private companies represent risky, illiquid investments, most acquirers of private companies seek a 15–30 per cent return on their investments, to compensate them with an appropriate 'premium'.

Thus, buyers have to be convinced that significant growth possibilities exist for them to pay a high multiple for your business. After all, a multiple of 10 times operating earnings implies only a 10 per cent pre-tax return on investment, just a slight premium to the 'riskless' return of Treasury Notes. No rational investor or acquirer would make that investment unless he was convinced that earnings could grow dramatically. Indeed, assuming a multiple of 10 times operating income, earnings would have to grow at a compound rate of 25 per cent over five years to provide the minimum 20 per cent annualized return on investment.

Comparisons are sometimes easier said than done. It is important to choose a universe of comparative companies that are similar in size, capitalization and industry. The problem is that the companies most like yours are typically other private companies, for which little or no public data exists. The same is true for sale transactions involving comparable private companies.

It is important to be very selective in comparing your operations with those of public companies. While data on these companies is readily available, most public companies will tend to be larger and more diversified than your own business. Markets tend to reward larger companies with higher multiples – primarily because they tend to have a breadth of products and a certain 'critical mass' that eludes most smaller, private companies. It is totally inappropriate for an owner of a £25 million manufacturer of test instruments to compare his operations with those of Hewlett-Packard.

In every comparison, you must be certain that you have enough facts on each company and its operations to make a sound judgement. For instance, you may know that your competitor sold for $40 million (£15 million). But without any more information than that, you are in no position to judge your own comparative value. Your competitor's business may have been more profitable than yours, it may have had a larger asset base or it may have had a significantly higher return on equity. Without a full understanding of those companies in your comparative universe, you must be somewhat wary of whatever conclusions result.

Value is always determined in the margin. If your neighbour's house recently sold for $415 000 (£250 000), everyone in your street will immediately adjust their internal expectations as to the value of their own houses. However, if everyone in your street suddenly put their house up for sale at the same time, prices would plunge from the weight of too much supply. Thus, it is the marginal deal, the last incremental deal, that sets value expectations for all.

Over the past two decades, small to mid-sized private companies have tended to trade in the range of 4–8 times current year recast operating earnings. In slow or difficult markets, the range has slid lower; in hot markets, the range has moved slightly higher. While the great majority of middle market deals are completed in this range, a good quarter of all deals trade higher or lower.

The market comparison approach assumes that a few recent deals are appropriate indicators of value. This may not always be the case. We recently sold a distributor of hydraulic components to a well-funded private equity group that was looking to consolidate in the field. The buyer paid a very high price for our client, as a cost of entry into the market. Once the group had purchased this company, however, they had established their presence in that region and were only interested in acquiring any other companies as 'add-on' acquisitions at substantially lower multiples. Thus, other distributors of hydraulic components may have wrongly used that transaction as a model of what values they could expect. Firms often pay 'premiums' to gain a foothold in a field, setting standards that no other parties in the field will subsequently match.

3. Income capitalization approach

The income capitalization approach is based on the present worth of the future economic benefits to be derived by an acquirer. Also called the 'discounted cash flow model', this approach attempts to determine the net present value of a company's expected future earnings stream over a certain 'payback' period. This method requires projections of future profits, based primarily on past results and assumptions as to future operating performance. These figures are then discounted back to a present value, using a discount rate competitive with rates of investments of comparable risk. (A discount rate is a rate at which annual future earnings are discounted to reflect the effects of inflation, the cost of money and the inherent risk of an investment.)

Most prospective buyers will tend to use some form of this model in assessing the value of your company. They will make their own judgements as to your future prospects and try to quantify those assessments into a set of projections. Most acquirers incorporate such factors as anticipated cost savings, synergies and new product development into their models. Obviously, these figures are never known by the seller.

The difficulty in preparing an income capitalization model is arriving at good, credible projections that all parties can live with. Sellers tend to be overly optimistic; buyers tend to be overly cautious. Buyers always believe that projections provided by sellers are suspect.

This method also involves important and often difficult judgements with regard to growth assumptions, cost savings, and the discount rate applied. Merger specialists have developed rather elaborate models to help you refine key variables in your projections, such as working capital needs and variable costs.

The strength of the income capitalization approach is that it examines your business the way most prospective buyers will: it looks to the future rather than to the past. The weakness is that its reliability depends on the quality and credibility of the projections.

EARNINGS

While the final determinate of your company's value may rest on a number of variables, your company's current and anticipated earnings stream is clearly the most important factor driving value. When an acquirer is willing to pay a 'premium' for your company, it is generally based on the assumption that your earnings will grow at above-market rates, either through efficiencies or synergies that the buyer brings to the deal.

The key to the value of most businesses is the ability to generate earnings. And yet, in order to minimize income taxes, many private company owners seek to suppress reported profits. Typical methods employed by owners to reduce taxable earnings include: generating inventory 'cushions' to minimize gross profits, expensing costs that should appropriately be capitalized, delaying the recognition of revenues into the next fiscal year, and expensing personal entertainment, meal, travel, vehicle and insurance costs through their companies. In addition, many owners draw compensation well in excess of what an outsider might term 'reasonable'. Thus, the financial statements of most private companies do not reflect the full earning capacity of these businesses.

In order to provide a true economic view of these companies, it is imperative to recast their financial statements to eliminate direct and indirect owner-related expenses, as well as expenses of an extraordinary, discretionary or non-recurring nature.

Because you want to identify all of the areas of potential profit enhancement, it is advisable to go through your operating statements on a line-by-line basis.

Most sophisticated acquirers will understand and accept the concept of re-stating your financial statements to reflect the 'true' profitability of your company. However, you will probably run into arguments over the extent and nature of some of your 'add-backs'.

First, buyers only recognize those add-backs that can be identified and documented; they will generally not accept those items that cannot be proven, such as hidden inventory or diverted cash. In addition, what you consider an unusual or 'non-recurring' expense may elicit a different response from a buyer. Professional fees and marketing costs are a normal, on-going part of doing business. Depreciation, too, is a legitimate cost of being in business, except in instances where depreciation costs are well above anticipated future capital expenditures (after all, you will eventually need to replace or upgrade your plant and equipment).

You should add-back to company income only that portion of officers' income that is excessive, not the entire amount. After all, someone has to be compensated to run the business.

Lastly, buyers will generally not pay you for efficiencies or synergies they bring to the table. Many sellers attempt to reconstruct their Profit/Loss statements based on what costs could be eliminated by combining with a prospective buyer. While these efficiencies or synergies may be very real, it is rare that a buyer will compensate you for what they bring to a deal. In most transactions, buyers value your business as a 'stand-alone' operation. Whatever efficiencies that accrue from a deal generally belong to the buyer.

MYTHS ABOUT VALUE

Ignoring conventional methods of valuation, many owners base their 'asking prices' on a number of myths and misconceptions about value. A few are outlined below.

1. The labour theory of value

Karl Marx developed this specious concept over 150 years ago. Some business owners would be horrified to know that they are unknowingly perpetuating it today.

In essence, the labour theory of value claims that a commodity's value should be based on the amount of labour that goes into producing it. Many owners wrongly believe that the value of their company should be directly related to the amount of work that they put into it. They tell us that they deserve a high price because of all of the sweat and toil they endured over the years.

This argument is akin to an artist who insists that his paintings should command high prices because he has spent years creating them. His art may fetch a high price, or it may not. Buyers will clearly value the art based on their own criteria, not by how much time the artist spent creating it.

The value of your business is independent of the many years you spent building it. The free enterprise system is based on market forces determining value, not labour content. Markets reward competence and creativity as evidenced by profits (or anticipated profits). The years it took to build your company is an irrelevant matter.

2. The revenue theory of value

Some owners suggest that extraordinary growth rates should command above-market values. That may be the case, but only if the growth is achieved with a commensurate increase in profitability.

It is not particularly impressive to grow sales at the expense of margins and profitability. The key is to grow sales profitably. Buyers tend to focus on the bottom line, not the top line. After all, you are generally paid multiples of earnings, not revenues.

3. The 'Just gimme my price' theory of value

A few owners ignore convention entirely and base their valuation assumptions on something more immediate: what they want to net from a deal. Regardless of the inherent strengths or weaknesses of their companies, these owners start the valuation process by first determining what they want from a deal, and then work backwards to justify that number.

A recent client demanded that his business be sold for $20 million, not based on any analytical study of the inherent merits of his company, but because he wanted to leave a certain amount to each of his children. This client actually spurned numerous offers of $15–18 million, even though those offers were presented with sound price justifications. To our knowledge, the company is still on the market. Businesses are valued on their inherent strengths and weaknesses, not an owner's whimsical desire to support his lifestyle or that of his progeny.

CONCLUSION

Too many owners place unrealistically high values on their businesses, because of either emotional attachments or non-objective assessments of their companies. In the end, you only wind up hurting yourself with unrealistic or insupportable expectations. Potential suitors may not even consider buying your business if they assume that a high asking price means that you are not serious about selling. Premium prices are occasionally paid for businesses, but you should never go through the time and effort of marketing your business expecting such a premium.

As we stated earlier, it is important that you establish value goals prior to marketing your company, if only to frame your reference of expectations. However, you need to keep in mind that this is only a starting point. Value is ephemeral; it is based on perception as much as fact. Many variables beyond the hard numbers will impact the eventual value of your business, including such intangible factors as your strengths, weaknesses and prospects, as well as the buyer's ultimate objectives.

FOUR

Issues to Address Before Considering a Sale

Once you have made a decision to sell, there are a number of preparatory actions you should take in order to make your company more attractive to potential buyers. Just as homeowners often remodel or repaint their houses to help them sell, business owners should take similar steps in preparing their companies for the market. As is true with most things in life, planning pays. By working through the following checklist of 'housekeeping chores', you will set the proper stage on which to market your company to outside parties. In addition, you may well significantly enhance the value of your business.

Initial impressions are very important in attracting and retaining the interest of potential suitors. Most of the actions that we outline in this chapter are aimed at satisfying prospective buyers' initial concerns, to make them comfortable enough to take a closer look. Over time, many companies develop policies and characteristics that are confusing or incomprehensible to others. It is difficult enough to convince potential acquirers to pay a premium price for your company; you need to help the process along by making your company as inviting and understandable as possible.

The 'housekeeping chores' that we suggest may take from two to 12 months to implement. In the end, however, the effort will be rewarded by the increased interest and value you will get for your company.

POSITION YOUR FINANCIAL STATEMENTS TO YOUR ADVANTAGE

The first place to start a programme of examination and correction is in the area of finance. After all, most decisions relating to value ultimately boil down to the past and potential earning power of your company. Thus, in contemplating a sale, it is vitally important that you first address how you can strengthen or better document your company's financial health.

Straighten out your financial affairs

Many private businesses are run more like sole proprietorships than public companies. Indeed, many owners operate their companies not to produce a stellar income statement for shareholders, but rather for their own personal benefit.

Most acquirers understand owners' desires to minimize taxable income. They accept many of the techniques owners employ to mask their earnings, such as accelerated depreciation, delaying recognition of revenue, expensing capital outlays, excessive compensation and owner perks. However, there are quite a number of tax-avoidance schemes that are of such a nature that they will 'turn off' prospective buyers. For example, owners of companies with a large 'cash' business can often divert some of the discretionary cash from the company straight into their own pockets. Alternatively, through the use of 'inventory cushions', or the deliberate undervaluing of inventory, owners are able to hide their profits from the taxman. You should not underestimate the negative impact of such questionable behaviour on a potential acquirer. Some buyers will walk away from a deal at the first sight of such illegal or unethical acts.

You should also be aware that such deliberate attempts to escape taxes may cause more than ethical dilemmas. Buyers will typically only recognize a company's traceable reconstructed profits; they will not pay for earnings that are not easily or clearly documented. Owners who have become adept at hiding profits from the tax authorities have the perverse challenge of having to prove to potential acquirers that those profits ever existed. Some owners have devised tax-avoidance schemes so complex that they can hardly recreate themselves what they did, let alone explain their actions to a prospective suitor.

The most direct way to deal with this dilemma is to 'invest in taxes' for a year or two. To prove that profits exist, you need to show them. Yes, this means that taxes will have to be paid (a horrible thought to some owners). But, given the fact that businesses are bought on a multiple of earnings, the investment of one year's taxes should reap multiples of that sum in a sale.

Likewise, you need to address the miscellaneous financial aspects of your business that have no direct bearing on your company's operations. If you have personal property or equipment on your company's books, or there are corporate assets you want to keep after the sale, like a large tract of undeveloped land adjacent to a facility, you should buy them or distribute them before you go to market. Their presence will just complicate and confuse matters later on.

Shareholder loans or inter-company receivables should be cleared up. Again, you do not want to make your balance sheet any more complicated than necessary.

You should also consider spinning off or eliminating marginal operations or subsidiary operations that are not central to your core business. We once worked with a client in the plastics-moulding business. The company also owned a small car-wash adjacent to one of its facilities. Though the owner loved his car-wash, it was clearly not germane to his plastics business. Potential buyers of his plastics company had no interest in also buying the car-wash. After several failed negotiations, we finally advised the client to spin off the car-wash to himself, in order to make a deal for the plastics company more palatable for suitors.

While this example may appear extreme, it certainly makes sense to remove from the buyer's consideration any unrelated businesses or assets, primarily so you do not steer the focus away from the core company.

Get audited statements

Having your financial statements audited, especially by one of the major accounting firms, increases a prospective buyer's faith in your company's financial position. Regardless of the terms of the deal, most prospective acquirers will have your books audited prior to buying your company. By providing potential suitors with audited statements at the outset, you accelerate the process and clear away one of the inevitable delays leading to a closing.

More importantly, by supplying suitors with audited numbers, you indicate your confidence that your figures are accurate and complete. Quite a number of very active buyers in today's marketplace, especially those that are public, refuse to consider any acquisition candidates that do not provide at least three years of audited statements.

You should be aware that an audit uncovers most games that owners play to mask profits. An arm's length financial audit will quickly shed light on profit-avoiding schemes such as 'inventory cushions'. Thus, an audit will force an owner to 'clean up his act', at least in terms of financial reporting. As we mentioned earlier, this may well prove to be beneficial in the increased confidence it gives the buyer.

Clean up your receivables and inventory

Over the course of a company's operating history, many owners become lax in policing their receivables and inventory. Receivables that have little chance of being collected are still carried at their original value. Inventory that is slow-moving or obsolete is not sufficiently marked down. We once had a client who insisted on carrying at full value a customized packaging job he had performed for a company long since bankrupt. Our client sincerely believed that some different customer would one day come calling for that precise job, and he would unload it all at full value.

Prior to buying your company, a prospective acquirer will send in his auditor to ferret out these problems. Most buyers will subtract any receivable or inventory problems from the purchase price, essentially giving you nothing for these assets. It makes more sense for you to address these problems yourself. That way, you have the time to either sort out the problems and salvage some value, or write them off and at least take the tax deduction for yourself.

POLISH YOUR PHYSICAL PLANT

While acquirers are primarily interested in the earnings power of your company, it is important to remember that you are also selling your physical assets. The condition of those physical assets says a tremendous amount about how you run your company and will definitely have an impact on any buyer's impression of your business. A cramped, run-down plant in a seedy part of town could by itself turn away prospective acquirers, even if your company mints money.

It behoves you to spend some time, effort and expense in making your physical plant as clean and presentable as possible prior to showing it to potential suitors. Specifically, you should carry out an inspection and effect any significant repairs or improvements that may be necessary, including:

- painting the exterior and interior walls;
- repairing or replacing all outmoded machinery or equipment;
- performing preventive maintenance on all other machinery and equipment;
- repairing road surfaces, clearing away rubble, and having the landscaping well-maintained;
- cleaning out the office, discarding all unnecessary papers and records that have accumulated;

- sprucing up or reconfiguring the offices to convey a warm, productive and efficient working environment.

No one expects your factory floor to be spotless; you obviously have to continue operating your business throughout the sale process. Some businesses tend to be cleaner than others; most suitors recognize that fact. However, a clean and crisp outward appearance displays both your and your employees' pride in your organization, and can have a favourable impact on prospective buyers.

A more vexing dilemma involves what to do if you are in dire need of a larger facility, a major piece of equipment or a new data processing system. The decision whether to proceed with these projects before selling or to leave those expenditures and headaches to the acquirer is not an easy one. In the end, it will boil down to a question of your desire to spend both the money and the effort to accomplish these tasks versus the incremental value these moves will add to your company.

Quite a number of business owners can clearly see significant benefits in expanding their capacity, but choose not to do so because they just do not want the hassle. On the other hand, we recently represented a distributor of electronic parts who clearly added significant value to his business by patiently waiting through the design, installation and debugging of a sophisticated inventory management system.

If you do decide to proceed with a major expansion of your plant or data processing system, you must be committed to seeing the project through to completion prior to selling. A company in the midst of a major plant renovation will appear too messy and uncertain a situation for most acquirers. To get any benefit from the time and expenditure involved, you must have both completed the expansion and operated smoothly for some period of time to demonstrate the tangible benefits of the expenditure.

CODIFY AND STRENGTHEN ANY CONTRACTUAL AFFAIRS

We once worked with a company that had a tradition of signing one-year labour contracts with its union every April Fool's Day. This tradition had been started by the former owner, who had a sense of humour about such things. The policy remained intact when the business was passed down to his son. While longer labour contracts might have been more sensible, each side seemed comfortable with the arrangement. There appeared to be no reason to change.

In fact, there was a very good reason to change: acquirers will most probably view such arrangements with disdain. It is very important to codify any contractual relationships your business has with outside parties. These relationships are a large part of what any acquirer is seeking; every buyer will want assurance as to some predictability and permanence of these relationships.

The most obvious relationships that need to be addressed are leases on plant and equipment, and labour contracts. Acquirers are interested in maintaining operating costs comparable to your present costs. You should try to negotiate long-term leases or contracts at or near historic costs; otherwise, acquirers may use the spectre of an increase in costs as a reason to justify a lower price.

It is unwise to consider selling just before a lease or labour contract expires. If the pending renegotiation does not frighten away a prospective buyer, the fear of the unknown liability will certainly dampen his enthusiasm and therefore his price. Better to negotiate the lease or contract yourself and provide the acquirer with predictable, known future costs.

Other considerations you should address are any formal contracts or informal relationships you have with suppliers or customers. If your company receives priority pricing from a vendor, or enjoys a special relationship with a customer, it would behove you to develop these situations into contractual affairs. A major concern of all potential acquirers will be that these relationships will end once they have bought the company and you have left.

STRAIGHTEN OUT YOUR RECORDS

Private business owners are notoriously poor at maintaining organized business records. Perhaps it is the lack of the discipline of a public market and its various regulatory bodies. Or, perhaps it is simply that owners see a greater use of their time in running their businesses than overseeing adequate record keeping.

Whatever the reason, it is imperative that you develop an accurate and complete accounting of all your business records prior to going to the market. Any potential acquirer will need to examine complete corporate records. It is certainly the sign of a well-disciplined, well-organized company to have its data available at the outset.

As a minimum, you should address the following areas of record keeping:

- articles of incorporation and minutes of directors' and shareholders' meetings;
- all documentation relating to compliance with various govern-mental regulations, including workers' compensation, retirement plans, workers' health and safety, environmental and equal oppor-tunity matters;
- tax records – you should be certain that you are not delinquent in any tax filings;
- leases and contracts binding the company – all should be executed and current;
- payroll records;
- documentation relating to patents, trademarks, or copyrights;
- documentation relating to distribution agreements, representation agreements, licensing agreements or franchise agreements;
- documentation relating to all bank loans and industrial revenue bonds.

BUILD A MANAGEMENT TEAM FOR TRANSITION

The single greatest asset that your company has is its people. Your hard assets do not generate earnings or market share; rather, your employees do. Therefore, potential acquirers want to know that the same people who developed your company for you will remain to run it for them.

A buyer's greatest fear is that the owner of a business flees town just after his business was acquired, leaving the buyer high and dry. It is imperative that you take the time to develop an experienced and dedicated management team before approaching suitors. Buyers not only want a commitment from an owner to remain for at least a transitional period, but they also like to see a competent second-tier of management, capable of one day assuming control. Buyers want to be made confident that the company can survive its owner.

Businesses that solely revolve around the abilities of their owners are very vulnerable. As far as possible, you should delegate respons-ibilities and decisions to subordinates, developing a broader base of abilities and experience within the company. The appearance of a phalanx of assertive, capable and dedicated managers anxious to grow the business will make your company much more attractive to buyers.

ESTABLISH ADEQUATE SYSTEMS AND CONTROLS

The presence of adequate information systems and financial controls can have a significant impact on the value of your company. Buyers are often quite willing to pay premiums for companies that have gone through the painful process of establishing sophisticated systems and controls. Not only can these companies provide quick responses to informational needs, but the buyers know that the information will be good, reliable data. In today's fast-changing business climate, the quick availability of reliable data is considered a necessary advantage.

More likely than not, you are not the best one to judge your internal systems and controls. Have your accounting firm, or better yet an outside consultant, review your data processing systems and financial controls to make certain that they are consistent with your needs. You may well find the cost and effort of updating your systems are repaid many times over.

ADDRESS ENVIRONMENTAL PROBLEMS

It is not at all uncommon for businesses today to be operating in violation of various national or local environmental regulations. From the use of an old underground oil tank to the disposal of caustic chemicals into a septic system, many businesses have policies or practices that need to be addressed. Unfortunately, many business owners are probably not even aware that their businesses are in violation of these regulations.

Because environmental problems can be so costly to clean up and because governing agencies are becoming increasing diligent in policing violators, quite a number of buyers today are demanding environmental audits prior to making acquisitions. Even the slightest problem can frighten away the most determined buyer, for fear that other, unknown liabilities exist.

You should take the time to carefully and systematically examine your production processes and facilities. You might even engage a qualified site inspector to give you his own assessment as to your environmental health.

We recently represented a client whose sale was delayed by five months while the copper that was found in the soil surrounding his plant was removed. Unbeknownst to the seller, the plant had been built during the American Civil War as a munitions factory. The copper was left over from the production of bullets! Needless to say, the prospective acquirer was quite upset by this late discovery, and its presence seriously threatened the deal. While the copper in the soil caused no threat to the environment, the regulatory authorities required that it be thoroughly removed before the transaction went through. Some foresight in discovering and cleaning up the soil before negotiations began would have led to a far smoother transaction.

Having your own audit prior to going to market allows you plenty of time both to locate actual or potential problems and to address the problems in the most cost-effective and efficient way. Most acquirers will want you to warrant that there are no environmental problems. If you have taken the time to inspect and fix the problems yourself, you will be in a far better position to do so.

CONCLUSION

To summarize: the key to preparing your business for sale is to look at your company from the perspective of the buyer and ask yourself, 'If I were buying this company, what would worry me?' Once you have honestly answered the question, take the necessary steps to remedy the situation. By going through such an introspective exercise, you will be well on your way to making your business more attractive to others.

How Intermediaries Fit into the Picture

In building your company, you have undoubtedly made invaluable contacts within your industry. Most probably you have also had numerous occasions to develop your negotiating skills, perhaps in acquiring one or more companies yourself. Thus, you would probably not be surprised that many business owners decide to sell their businesses by themselves. Yet, as the old saying goes, a doctor who performs surgery on himself has a fool for a patient. Our experience shows that the same can be said about a business owner who attempts to sell his own business.

Selling a business can be a very complex and time-consuming proposition. There are many legal, tax, accounting and regulatory issues to address. In addition, there is the matter of finding the appropriate buyer for your company, and then negotiating and structuring the most advantageous deal for yourself.

The sale of your business could well be the most important economic decision you make. To help you arrange the best transaction for your needs, you should consider using a qualified professional merger intermediary to guide you through the sale process. After all, the cost of good advice is cheap compared to the cost of a serious error of judgement.

An intermediary (also called a broker, merger adviser or an investment banker) is essentially an agent authorized to act for you in arranging a transaction. Intermediaries can act for either buyers or sellers; often, both sides of a deal will engage their own advisers. The basic role of an intermediary is to search for appropriate acquisition candidates for his client and then negotiate and structure a deal. An intermediary works with his client throughout the sale process, from devising the initial strategy to seeing the transaction through to close. It is important to note that while an intermediary represents his client's interests in the market, he is not in a legal position to commit his client to anything.

Intermediaries are not to be confused with finders, whose main purpose is to introduce two parties in the hope of creating a deal, for which a fee is paid. Finders generally play a limited role in any transaction; they are not representatives for one side or the other. Rather, they are working for the 'deal'. Finders simply bring two parties together with the idea of fostering a transaction.

Leaving finders aside, there are many reasons to use an intermediary in selling your business, including the following.

Experience

It has taken you years to develop the skills necessary to build a successful company. Likewise, a competent intermediary has spent years developing an understanding of and experience in the field of mergers and acquisitions. A professional intermediary brings to a transaction an intimate knowledge of both the current market and the acquisition process, and can help you to properly price and package your company. A competent intermediary also has the skills necessary to handle the technical aspects of a sale, including structuring a transaction to meet your objectives and advising on evolving tax, legal, accounting and regulatory issues.

Objectivity

Company owners often have large emotional stakes in their businesses, which hinder their objectivity in both valuing their companies and negotiating sale transactions. It is difficult for an owner to separate himself from his emotions in selling his business. Better to let an intermediary represent your interests in the market, if nothing more than to provide an independent perspective on the process.

Knowledge of buyers

You may believe that you already know your likely acquirers: your competitors. Yet frequently, much higher values come from buyers outside your specific industry. An intermediary can provide your company with exposure to a much broader range of potential suitors, including foreign multinational firms, large and small domestic companies and private investor groups. Because of their stature in the market and their experience, merger advisers can often get better access to corporate officers and key 'decision makers' than you can yourself.

Confidentiality

Most owners contemplating a sale want to be certain that the matter is handled as discreetly and confidentially as possible. A leak to key employees, customers or suppliers could cause a significant disruption of business. In general, the more direct contact between you and potential acquirers, the greater the chance that the confidentiality of the project will be violated.

It is the role of an intermediary to initiate and maintain all contact with potential acquirers. By orchestrating and controlling the sale from a remote site, an intermediary insulates you from any direct exposure to buyers until the proper time. Through judicious screening of buyers and the use of strong non-disclosure agreements, a competent intermediary should be able to maintain confidentiality throughout the sale process.

Skill at negotiations

More likely than not, the eventual buyer of your business will have been through the acquisition process numerous times before encountering you. You, on the other hand, probably have limited experience in such matters. Thus it is vitally important that you have an expert in your corner, not only to negotiate the best terms, but to structure the transaction so that it meets your personal, financial and corporate needs. Because an intermediary has no legal authority to commit on your behalf, he can actually give you an advantage, always having to check with you before agreeing to anything. This allows you to preserve your flexibility and gives you the 'upper hand' in negotiations. The evolving laws regarding tax, accounting and estate planning issues are another prime reason to engage an expert to guide you through this complex maze.

Role as a buffer

Because a buyer and seller often end up working together in some form after the acquisition, it is important to develop and maintain a positive relationship throughout the sale process. Yet this is often difficult to do when the two principals are negotiating for themselves. An intermediary acts as a buffer between the two parties, allowing each to negotiate tough deals, yet avoiding direct confrontation. When discussions reach an impasse, an intermediary can often suggest alternative solutions to keep the dialogue going. The presence of a third party in negotiations can prompt candour and lessen tensions between you and the buyer. In addition, an intermediary can cast your company in the best light to a potential acquirer, in a way that might appear improper or egotistical for an owner to do himself.

The sale of a business is a very time-consuming process. An intermediary's role is to relieve you of most of the burdens and pressures associated with the sale of your business. You need to stay active and informed of the selling process, because, in the end, you will make all of the decisions. However, if an intermediary has properly fulfilled his role, your involvement in the details of the sale should be minimal.

Although each situation is unique, an intermediary generally handles the following functions:

- determines the advisability of a sale and potential value ranges;
- develops an appropriate selling strategy, including preparing a listing of potential domestic and foreign buyers;
- prepares a descriptive memorandum, describing in full detail your company's operations and prospects;
- contacts potential acquirers, with a discreet and selective approach;
- schedules and conducts meetings with suitors;
- maintains dialogue with potential acquirers, providing necessary information and market data;
- negotiates the price and other terms;
- works the transaction through until closing, including helping to prepare the sale contract.

While a competent, professional intermediary can add great value to the sale process, an ill-informed, inexperienced adviser can cause more harm than good. After a while, the market will come to associate your company with your intermediary, and essentially view them as one entity. If your adviser has a poor reputation or no experience in acquisitions, it reflects poorly on you. Of course, the ultimate harm from an incompetent intermediary will be the poor advice he might give. Thus, you should look for the following characteristics in choosing a professional to represent you and your company.

Professionalism

An intermediary's reputation can have a profound impact on how your company is viewed by the market. Certain merger advisers have such poor reputations that many buyers simply refuse to work with them, regardless of the merits of their clients. Be certain that your adviser has the background and credentials to do the job for you.

Experience

Nothing succeeds like success, and you certainly do not want someone 'cutting his teeth' on the sale of your company. Check to make certain that an intermediary has a history of successfully initiating and completing deals involving companies of a similar size and nature as yours. Active intermediaries are more respected in the market; they tend to generate more interest in their clients. Go with a proven winner.

Focused effort

The sale of your business is important to you; you want it to be important to your adviser. Make certain that the intermediary you choose will give your project the proper amount of attention and effort. Try to avoid intermediaries that take a 'listings' approach: working on dozens of companies concurrently in the hope that one will sell. While the 'numbers game' may work for them, you need a hard-working adviser dedicated to seeing your project through to a successful transaction. Good deals do not just happen; they require hard work and persistence on the part of your adviser. Find an intermediary who shares this credo.

Senior level attention

Check to find out who will be working on your project within the merger advisory firm. Many investment banks pass on smaller deals to junior associates; large 'listings' firms employ dozens of account executives, many of whom were selling insurance or stocks in a prior career. They may have little or no experience in selling companies. The sale of your business is important to you. Find a merger advisory firm that is anxious enough about working on your sale to devote a senior level partner to oversee your project.

Sensitivity to your objectives

Just as no two private company owners are alike, no two owners' objectives are alike. The adviser you choose to represent your interests must be willing to take the time to completely understand your personal, financial and corporate goals. The intermediary should then be willing to tailor his approach to meet those objectives. There is no such thing as a standardized marketing effort; do not even consider those advisers who refuse to conform to your wishes.

Representing only sellers

Many investment banks handle a wide variety of corporate finance activities, including trading and underwriting stock and bond issues. In the same vein, many merger intermediaries work both sides of the street: they offer merger advisory services to both buyers and sellers. This situation can cause significant conflicts of interests, especially for the seller of a private company. Buyers are constantly in the market for deals, which can represent multiple fees for a merger adviser. As a seller, you will only ever represent one fee. Conflicting loyalties can not make an intermediary a true advocate of the seller.

The best way to avoid this conflict of interest is to work with an intermediary who only represents sellers in the market. If that is not possible, at least discuss the possible conflicts with your prospective adviser to determine how he plans to deal with the issue.

Personal compatibility

Because the selling process includes work that is alternately tedious and tense, it is important that you get along well with your adviser. You are going to depend on your adviser greatly. You should be certain from the outset that the 'chemistry' is right, and that there are no personality conflicts.

SELECTING AN INTERMEDIARY

Businesses do not sell themselves; the best buyers rarely find you without an active marketing effort. For that reason, the intermediary you employ has to be both experienced and aggressive. To be certain that you choose the best adviser consistent with your goals, interview several potential intermediaries and check their references carefully. Intermediary firms vary greatly in size and scope – from 'one-man shops' to large investment banks. Make certain that the firm you choose has all of the capabilities you require, while being focused enough to give you top-level attention and service.

You should be very selective in choosing your merger adviser, just as you would in hiring a lawyer or accountant. Many business libraries, local chambers of commerce and industry associations have directories of active merger advisers; however, such listings should only serve as a start to your search. Seek suggestions and recommendations from friends, business associates and competitors who have sold their businesses. Personal recommendations are obviously the most reliable source of leads. By discreetly asking around and doing some home-work, you should be able to develop a short-list of competent, active intermediaries.

Once you have narrowed the universe down to a select few, you should take the time to individually interview each candidate, weighing the relative strengths and weaknesses of each one. Experi-enced merger advisers should understand your desire to engage in such a 'beauty pageant'; do not even consider those that will not participate in such a selection process.

As an integral part of your interviewing process, you should ask all candidates to provide references of recent clients whose businesses the intermediary has sold. Call these references and ask detailed questions about the process and their experience with that inter-mediary. Completed deals are a merger adviser's only tangible evidence of success; it behoves you to take the effort to vet the record of your prospective adviser and partner in this journey.

Lastly, you should be aware of situations where an intermediary representing a potential buyer approaches you on his client's behalf. At first, this situation might appear ideal: you can sell your company without going through the difficult process of marketing it, while saving yourself a fee to an intermediary. It is important to remember, however, that the investment banker approaching you is looking out for his client's interests, not yours, and therefore cannot be counted on to provide proper or even reliable advice. Also, while this situation may well by-pass the effort of marketing your company and an inter-mediary's fee, it could well cost you dearly in the long run. You wind up negotiating with only one party (perhaps not even a very strong one), without the benefit of any professional advice.

TERMS AND FEES

Most merger intermediaries work on contingent fees: they are paid a pre-arranged percentage of the total purchase price if and when a deal closes. These arrangements are typically best for the seller – a fee is paid only if the intermediary is successful in selling the company. This arrangement tends to align an intermediary's interests with those of his client: both have an interest selling the company at the highest possible price.

Fees are generally based on a sliding scale of between 2 and 5 per cent on transactions in the range $5–75 million (£3–45 million). Inter-mediaries may also ask for retainers to be paid at the commencement of their activities, to cover their overhead, and any direct expenses incurred. If a retainer is to be paid, it should be netted from any eventual contingent fee, and should be modest in size. No intermediary should make money on a retainer – his profit should come only by successfully selling his client's company.

It is customary for professional intermediaries to ask you to enter into a written brokerage agreement, generally for a six-month period. Statues of frauds generally require brokerage agreements to be in writing to be enforceable. It is best for you to enter into a formal agreement so that both sides fully understand the terms under which the intermediary will develop and implement a strategy to sell your business.

An 'exclusive agreement' provides the intermediary with the exclusive right to offer a company for sale; the intermediary will receive a fee if any transaction occurs during the term of the agreement, whether the intermediary introduced the buyer or not. A 'non-exclusive agreement' requires the seller to pay the intermediary a fee only if the intermediary introduces the party that makes the acquisition.

The most successful intermediaries generally only work on an exclusive basis. Those that will work on a non-exclusive basis will still devote more time and effort to those clients who have given them an exclusive sale mandate. It is important to remember that intermediaries have businesses to run and must allocate their limited time to various clients. They will clearly put greater efforts behind those clients that have made the commitment to work exclusively with them.

It is much more difficult to maintain confidentiality and control of a sale process if you do not have one single adviser coordinating and implementing the process. In the end, it is probably best to choose the intermediary with whom you are most comfortable and give them a fair shot at selling the business through an exclusive agreement.

Because the selling process is a collaborative effort, you can help to achieve a swift sale by working closely with your adviser and being totally candid about your business, its problems and its prospects. You should never circumvent your adviser by concealing possible prospects or dealing directly with those prospects yourself. This only serves to undermine your intermediary's efforts, and can prove to be very counter-productive. Once you have engaged an intermediary, assume the fee is a given and work closely with your adviser to achieve the best possible deal.

The Sale Process

Selling your business is not unlike the sale of any other product. You need to understand your product, convey its attractiveness to others, get to know the needs and wants of your prospective buyer, and sell, sell, sell.

The basic principles remain the same as in any selling situation. There are no shortcuts, and rewards usually go to those willing to put in the effort. Most importantly, you can only succeed if you constantly pay attention to your customer (in this case, the potential buyer of your company).

The owner who recognizes the need for adequate preparation and effort in selling his business will go a long way toward ensuring the ultimate sale of his company at an attractive price. On the other hand, the owner who approaches the sale in an aloof or indifferent manner will tend to find that he will not attract any buyers for his company, regardless of price.

A commitment of considerable time and effort on your part is required both to maximize the value for your business and to find the 'right' buyer. The sale of your business is as important an economic decision as any you will face. It should command at least the same allocation of your time and resources as any other major project. If you are unwilling to commit these resources, if the goal does not seem worth the effort, then you should seriously reconsider selling your business.

The first step in selling your business is to make the commitment to sell. Most sophisticated buyers only want to expend efforts on opportunities where they sense a sincere interest in selling. There are enough attractive opportunities in the market that good buyers generally do not need to waste their time chasing 'tyre kickers' or sellers who are not really serious.

There are literally thousands of private businesses today that are perpetually 'for sale'. Many owners take the stance that 'anything is for sale at the right price'. These owners are continually willing to entertain all suitors that approach them. Yet, without any true desire to sell their companies, these owners go about the process in a haphazard, disinterested manner and generally find their efforts unrewarded. After a while, these companies tend to be tagged as 'shop worn' or as 'used goods'.

Nothing is as attractive the second time around. Many of the best suitors refuse to even consider companies that are perpetually 'for sale', on the market for all-comers. Most buyers assume that these companies must have some unattractive feature which prevented their sale to earlier suitors. After a while, owners of these businesses have essentially spoiled the market for their companies. When the time comes that they really want or need to sell, they will probably find that the only interested parties are 'opportunistic' buyers, those who will only buy at distressed prices.

An extreme example of this occurred a few years ago to an owner of a company that manufactured lighting fixtures. On the off-chance that a buyer might pay an outrageous amount for his business, this owner was open to discussing the sale of his business with anyone who approached him. Eventually, word leaked throughout his industry that he was for sale, but only at an unrealistic price. A number of his competitors approached him about buying his company, only to be turned off by his unprofessional presentation and unrealistic expectations. Most, however, never went near, believing that the deal had become 'shop worn'.

Three years after we first met this owner, he was told that he had developed cancer. At this point, he became desperate to sell. Yet, though we were retained to do an exhaustive search for a buyer, we could find no takers. We eventually had to cobble together a very unsatisfactory sale to his employees, which left the company burdened with debt and the owner with most of his proceeds in seller notes. The company was basically healthy and had a bright future; the main impediment to a successful sale was the stigma of being 'over-shopped'.

In our experience, few businesses actually sell because of chance meetings or direct approaches made by buyers. The best deals generally do not chase after you. Rather, you have to be aggressive in seeking them out. A proper sale of a business requires a tremendous amount of effort: preparing presentation materials, generating a universe of qualified buyers, making approaches, coordinating visits and negotiating and structuring deals. Most attempts to circumvent this effort only lead to dashed expectations or poor deals.

You are only going to sell your business once; it certainly makes sense that you do it right the first time.

Once you have decided to commit yourself to the long, arduous process of selling your business, there is a well-defined set of steps you can take to improve your chances of arranging a successful sale of your company.

1. ESTABLISH YOUR GOALS AND STRATEGIES

To properly address a sale of your business, you need to first establish a detailed, prioritized list of goals you want to achieve. By going through this introspective exercise, you may be surprised to find what goals are truly important to you, both personally and in terms of your company. It is clearly better to have confronted and thought through the many issues and questions involved in a sale before approaching potential buyers. Not only will this allow you to respond better to a buyer's demands, but it will impact the strategy you employ in seeking out potential buyers in the first place.

Issues that every potential seller should address range from the very broad to the very detailed, and probably should at least include the following:

- What are your main reasons for considering a sale? What do you want personally from a sale? What do you want for your company?
- What characteristics are you looking for in an acquirer?
- Do you want to remain with your company after a sale? Only for a transitional period or indefinitely to oversee growth?
- What deal structure helps you to achieve your financial goals? An all-cash deal? A tax-deferred stock swap? Are you willing to accept terms in exchange for a higher price?
- Do you have children in the business and what continued role do you see for them?
- Do you want to retain the land and property separately or sell them with the business?
- Do you feel any financial or other obligations to your management team? Employees?
- Would it matter if an acquirer moved your business or merged your business into theirs?
- How important is confidentiality to you? How vital is it that your employees and customers not know that you are for sale?

Some owners want to maximize the value they receive for their companies, regardless of who the buyers are. Others are unwilling to consider foreign acquirers, even if it means forgoing higher prices for their companies. Some owners want to retain the autonomous integrity of their companies; others do not care if their businesses are moved or employees are fired.

You should seek advice from others to help you think through these various issues, especially from your family, financial advisers and business associates. You should also seek out those business owners who have already sold their companies, both to get a better understanding of how they handled the process and also to learn from their experiences and mistakes. Only by going through such self-examination and general fact gathering can you determine what you really want from a sale.

Having sorted out your goals, you next need to develop a strategy to achieve them. Our experience shows that few successful deals result from a haphazard approach to selling. You need to address the sale of your company with a coordinated plan from the outset.

A well-conceived strategy will force you to define the types of acquirers you want to approach, the method of sale you want to employ, and the timetable you want to set to accomplish the sale.

If one of your main goals is to keep your management team in place and reward them for their efforts in building your company, you might want to consider first offering the company to them in a management buyout. Management buyouts often require some seller financing and rarely offer owners the best economic deal, but they are a preferred way for many company owners to reward faithful employees.

Alternatively, if your prime goal is to cash in at the highest possible price, then you should probably pursue a strategy of approaching a broad base of potential buyers to let the 'market' determine the highest bidder.

You need to establish an anticipated schedule at the outset, and continually monitor your progress against this timetable. A typical sale, if properly employed, should take from six to nine months to complete. Table 6.2 at the end of this chapter outlines a typical timetable and chronology of the sales process.

As with any forward planning, you need to be flexible and reasonable in your plans and expectations. Markets are constantly changing; so too might your company's operating performance or future prospects. You must be nimble enough to change your plans with changing conditions. By taking a planned but flexible approach to selling your company, you will go a long way towards assuring a successful deal.

2. PREPARE PRESENTATION MATERIALS

Many owners honestly believe that by simply announcing to the marketplace that their businesses are for sale, they can sit back and wait for the generous offers to come cascading in. Nothing could be further from the truth. The most active buyers are constantly deluged with acquisition proposals. Beset with so many opportunities, many buyers choose to pursue only those situations that are clearly and succinctly presented to them. Because it is difficult enough to get a deal done in the best of circumstances, most buyers will shy away from any situation where they are not provided with a complete and understandable description of the business at the outset.

Your company will be one of dozens of similar companies for sale at any given time; you need to make your company stand out from the crowd, to differentiate your company from all the other, mundane opportunities out there. You also need to provide potential acquirers with the relevant data they need to make a rational, informed decision on whether or not to pursue the acquisition of your company. For these reasons, it is important that you and your advisers prepare a complete descriptive memorandum on your company before going to market. Not only will such a memorandum provide a detailed understanding of your business, it will indicate a sincere and professional approach to selling your company.

One of an intermediary's most important roles is preparing a professional selling memorandum on your company, presenting your company in its best light and highlighting those points he knows will impress buyers.

If there are problems or weaknesses (as there are with most companies), the memorandum will provide you with a forum to address them from your point of view. A descriptive memorandum also allows you an opportunity to explain and highlight certain features of your financial statements, including a re-casting of both your income statements and your balance sheet.

Presenting a descriptive memorandum on your company makes it easy for a prospective buyer to move to the next stage; he has enough of the facts at the outset to make an informed decision on whether or not to pursue your company.

A sample table of contents from a descriptive memorandum is provided in Table 6.1. The idea is to clearly and succinctly describe your business, both its current operations and its future prospects.

It is vital that you provide a detailed analysis of your company, including a listing of your largest customers and suppliers (by volume), your employees (by compensation and length of service) and your facilities. Any acquirer will demand this information before bidding on your company; it makes sense to provide it to them at the outset.

Some owners actually go to the opposite extreme, providing in excruciating detail all possible data on their operations. Given the short

Table 6.1

Sample table of contents for a descriptive memorandum

attention span of most people, we believe that this is as b
as not having a prospectus on your company at all.

The objective of a descriptive memorandum is not to c
a suitor with information, but rather to make it easy to find th
data on your company. You want the memorandum to be i   ...gn,
but it should also be streamlined, no more than 20–35 pages of text.
The offering prospectus should be written so that it can be read in 15–
20 minutes.

Be certain that the data you include in the descriptive memorandum is true, accurate and complete. Various potential buyers will
make decisions and, ultimately, offers based on the information
provided in the memorandum. To the extent that any of it is misleading,
inaccurate, or incomplete, it will undermine your credibility, and could
eventually jeopardise any deal that you had negotiated. We always
advise clients that it is best to make full disclosure at the outset. Any
potential buyer will eventually unearth all of the facts: better to gain
their trust by disclosing everything at the beginning.

In the end, having a complete descriptive memorandum on your
company will aid you in screening potential acquirers and also enable
you to conserve your time. After all, if a suitor wants to meet you after
reviewing the material, you know that he is attracted enough by the
basics of your business to warrant going to the next step. Conversely,
those parties no longer interested in your business after reviewing
the memorandum will not waste your time with introductory meetings.

3. IDENTIFY PROSPECTIVE BUYERS

Over the years, most owners have probably given some thought to
an informal list of prospective buyers of their companies. This list
generally includes competitors, suppliers or customers. At times it may
also include contacts made either socially or through various trade
functions.

You may believe that one of your competitors would be the logical
acquirer of your business; after all, a competitor should be able to justify
a higher price by simply eliminating duplication of overhead. At times,
that occurs. Yet, more often than not, your competitors are not the
logical acquirers of your business.

Competitors often believe that they can expand their market share
at a cost greatly below that of buying your company. In addition,
competitors already know all of the problems and difficulties of
your industry, and that often clouds their optimism. Consequently,

competitors often end up being low bidders for your business. On top of that, by engaging in discussions with competitors, you allow them open access to your operations, employees and strategies. This can be a real detriment if a deal does not go through with them.

We have found that those who are most willing to 'pay up' for companies are those who are presently outside your field (or, at best, peripherally involved in it) but have become convinced that your industry is one in which they want to expand. These buyers are often willing to pay a premium as a cost of entry into a new area. Your company can offer an immediate presence in a new market. The costs and risks of buying an established business are significantly less than the costs and risks of starting from scratch in a new field.

Thus, you should expand your search beyond the obvious. The financial markets today are global in nature, and you should broaden your range of potential buyers to include as many different parties from as many different perspectives as possible.

Because of their presence in the marketplace, competent inter-mediaries will have a good understanding of active buyers and their acquisition criteria. Your financial advisers should be able to glean through a large universe of potential acquirers to compile a list appropriate for you, including foreign multinational companies, large and small domestic companies, private investor groups and owner-managers who are looking for businesses to buy and run.

The ultimate list of appropriate potential candidates will depend greatly on your company and your goals. Large, synergistic corpo-rations obviously offer you and your company different alternatives than private investor groups. You need to work closely with your advisers to generate a group of potential buyers that appear to best fit your needs and desires. Obviously, your advisers should screen all potential suitors to make certain that their interests coincide with yours, and that they have the financial wherewithal to complete a deal.

Even if you do decide to include your competitors in your search, you should approach those potential buyers outside your industry first, before engaging in any conversations with competitors. Those outside your industry will need more time to understand and get comfortable with your business. By approaching them first, you give them a head start in their preliminary groundwork. Additionally, in dealing with suitors that are outside your industry, you are better able to control confidentiality. You want to minimize your exposure to leaks; those outside your industry will probably treat these matters with more discretion than those in your own field of business.

Only after you garner interest and offers from unrelated parties should you ever consider going to your competitors. With offers already in your pocket, you have tremendous leverage in getting competitors to move quickly and to act decisively. You force your competitors to make a quick decision on buying your business, lest you sell to one of the unrelated parties. This approach allows competitors minimal time to make use of confidential information or cause leaks in the market. It will also give you the upper hand in negotiating an advantageous deal from them.

4. CREATE A MARKET

There are a number of different methods you can employ to sell your business, from approaching each potential acquirer separately to orchestrating an open auction. Each method has its own strengths and weaknesses.

In our experience, the best way to sell is to create a market for your business. By creating a market, you allow the competitive nature of the market to play one bidder against another to generate the highest possible price. A competitive market also presents you with an array of prospective acquirers, allowing you to weigh the relative strengths and weaknesses of each suitor.

By talking to only one party at a time, you put yourself at a competitive disadvantage. A solitary suitor will clearly know that he is the only one examining your company, and will consequently feel less compelled to offer a good deal on acceptable terms. You have little leverage in negotiating with a solitary buyer – you either accept their proposal or walk away from the deal. Additionally, even if a lone party offered you a tremendous deal, it is difficult to gauge the relative value of the offer in a vacuum, without other competing bids. In a market environment, you gain all of the leverage. Potential buyers have to step up with attractive offers at the outset, lest they lose the deal to more aggressive suitors.

The truest way to openly market your company is through the auction process. This generally involves contacting and circulating as many offering memoranda to as many suitors as possible, with bids due by a prescribed date. Those whose initial bids are deemed acceptable are allowed to visit the management at the company facilities prior to making a final, binding offer.

The upside to this process is that it gives your company the widest possible exposure, often generates the highest prices, and quickly, efficiently gets the job done. The potential problems with an auction, however, are many:

- When circulating so many memoranda (sometimes up to 500), confidentiality is almost impossible to maintain. In fact, to get as many potential buyers to participate as possible, auctions are often announced publicly.
- With confidential operating and strategic data released to so many parties, competitors will almost always walk away from an auction having gained significant new information on the selling company.
- The entire process is demoralizing and disruptive to management and employees.
- Many of the more sophisticated buyers refuse to participate in openly competitive 'bid' situations. Ironically, an auction often frightens away the very buyers you want to attract.

The gravest problem with an auction is that once you start down the path, it is extremely difficult to change direction. The pressures are tremendous to accept whatever the highest offer is, whether attractive or not. After all, you have shown your hand to your competition. Your suppliers and customers are all expecting a change in ownership. And, if the sale process is terminated, your management and employees will never completely trust you again. They will continually wonder when you are next going to put the company up for sale.

A middle ground does exist between talking to one party and auctioning your company: the controlled sale. Essentially, a controlled sale attempts to blend the control and confidentiality of dealing with a single suitor with the market mechanisms of an auction. With a controlled sale, the idea is to have four to six parties concurrently examining and bidding for your business. To cull the four to six interested suitors may take 50 approaches, but that still causes less exposure and distraction than approaching 500. A skilled intermediary should be quite capable of generating a universe of 50 highly likely suitors.

Through a controlled sale, confidentiality and discretion are maintained, and yet you still benefit from a market environment. You can still play one bidder off against another. And, if you properly choose your suitors and orchestrate the process correctly, you will be able to generate values which should approximate those on an 'open' market.

There are two important points you should remember in creating a market for your company:

(a) *Use a third party to make the initial approaches.* There is nothing discreet about you approaching someone to buy your company. Regardless of what you say or how you say it, you are approaching him with hat in hand. It is always better to have a third party, preferably a skilled professional, make the approaches for you. By making 'blind' approaches, initially seeking out a prospective buyer's appetite for acquisitions, a third party is able to maintain your confidentiality until interest is expressed. Also, a third party acts as a buffer between you and the potential acquirers, allowing you to maintain some degree of autonomy and leverage. Lastly, the process of making approaches and interfacing with an array of suitors can become very time-consuming. Your efforts are better spent profitably running your business.

(b) *Make use of confidentiality agreements.* Confidentiality agreements (or non-disclosure agreements) are essentially agreements by a prospective buyer to not disclose either: 1) that your company is for sale, or 2) any of the data on your company that will be provided. We always insist that any potential acquirer executes a confidentiality agreement before the name of our client or any other information is divulged. (Copies of two sample confidentiality agreements are given in Appendix I.)

You should be aware that confidentiality agreements are difficult to enforce. The onus is on you, the seller, to prove a breach of the agreement, and then to prove damages. It is generally very difficult to trace the exact source of any leak, let alone to prove damages. However, a confidentiality agreement does achieve a more limited goal: it sends a clear signal to any potential suitor that you consider the information you are providing to be confidential, and that you expect it to be treated as such. Generally, those who are experienced in mergers and acquisitions respect the confidential nature of any data provided to them. Confidentiality problems generally come from smaller, less sophisticated groups with little experience in mergers and acquisitions.

5. SELL, SELL, SELL

The key to getting a suitor interested in your business is to get them excited about its prospects. Interest and value are often based on perception. Psychologists have shown that first impressions often determine one's ultimate perception of a situation. Fortunately, you can have a great deal of influence over how your company is perceived.

After a potential buyer expresses an interest in your business, he will undoubtedly want to arrange a visit to meet you face-to-face and to examine your facilities. Use this first visit as an opportunity to further excite the suitor about your business.

There are a number of things you can do to make certain that your buyer meetings are successful, including:

- Get acquainted with the potential acquirer and their current operations before the meeting, so you appear informed and interested in them.
- Understand the suitor's acquisition criteria, so you can tell them why your operation could fit well with theirs.
- Set an agenda with the potential acquirer prior to the meeting, so that you are properly prepared to cover all of the issues that are important to them.
- Learn from your adviser what concerns, if any, the potential acquirer has expressed about your business, so that you can address them at the meeting.
- Be open and honest. Most acquirers have been through the process more than once and can sense when they are not getting the full story. Stubbornness at providing key company data generally signals to buyers that you are hiding something. You need to establish credibility at the outset. All businesses have problems or weaknesses; be prepared to discuss yours fairly and openly.
- Do not be suspicious. Potential acquirers may ask you a tremendous number of questions, from the significant to the obscure. Have patience and answer them as fully and honestly as possible. You would probably ask the same questions and want to get the same amount of detail if you were about to pay a lot of money for a business.

We once had a client who insisted that no potential buyer was more important than the actual running of his business. Consequently, he insisted on taking phone calls in the middle of buyer meetings and ducking out of plant tours to work at his desk. He was generally unprepared for most meetings, citing his backlog of work. Our client's skewed sense of priorities only harmed himself in the long-term. Though the owner had built a fine second-tier of management capable of running his company, potential buyers got the mistaken impression that the business was too dependent on our client to ever be passed on to a new owner. Consequently, our client lost the interest of most likely suitors.

One of the major concerns of any prospective buyer is that you are selling because of some imminent problem with your business, like massive customer defections or product obsolescence. You need to be sympathetic to this concern and go to great lengths to make the buyer feel comfortable with the long-term prospects of your business.

In the end, it is imperative that you present your company in the best light to make it attractive to others. Any selling you do should be subtle, but you need to sell none the less. There is no product, nor any company, that truly sells itself.

KEEPING THE BUSINESS GOING

While you are going through the sale process, there are two matters on the home front that you need to address: your employees and your business.

With regard to your employees, we generally suggest informing only those employees who need to know of your plans. By announcing your plans to sell before a deal is at hand, you will create tremendous insecurity and disruption among your workforce, not to mention your customers and suppliers.

Once a deal is announced, the employees will know all about the acquirer, which will go a long way in making them more secure and comfortable about their futures. It is in the period between the decision to sell and the announcement of a deal, when the future is so uncertain, that employees are so concerned about their own security.

If a sale is conducted properly, you should be able to go through the process without employees ever finding out. Conduct plant tours under a guise, and have meetings and phone conversations off-site. The only way that your employees will have suspicions is if you start to act suspiciously.

With regard to your business, you need to continue to operate for the long term, as if no sale were going to occur. The most obvious reason for this is that the sale process may fail. Given the possibility that you may continue to own your company, it obviously makes sense for you to keep it running as well as possible.

Too many owners take their eyes off running of their company in anticipation of sale. This is a grave mistake. You need to keep your business operating at peak performance throughout the process to demonstrate its worth to suitors. Nothing can impair your chances of maximizing value more than showing disappointing operating results in the middle of negotiations. Remember, interest and value are often based primarily on perception. If your profits or prospects drop, so too will your company's value and your negotiating strength.

There is a temptation for owners to sacrifice the future for the present. In an effort to show attractive earnings, many owners curtail necessary spending on such things as advertising and development, and raise prices to show immediate margin increases. Yet, such

Table 6.2

Typical timetable/chronology of the sales process

Month 1

- Select intermediary; work with adviser in collecting necessary data
- Adviser prepares selling memorandum
- Adviser develops an approach list of potential acquirers
- Discuss and approve approach list and strategy with adviser

Months 2–3

- Adviser makes approaches
- Discuss and screen responses with adviser
- Have confidentiality agreements executed by interested parties
- Provide memorandum and other necessary data

Month 4

- Adviser arranges plant tours and management interviews
- Continue to expand candidate list and make new approaches
- Continue to provide data to interested parties

Months 5–6

- Adviser generates initial offers
- Cull offers and determine parties to pursue
- Adviser receives additional offers from potential acquirers
- Adviser provides expanded data and arranges follow-up facility visits
- Adviser negotiates between various suitors to elicit highest offers
- Evaluate various offers with adviser
- Decide on a deal
- Negotiate and execute a letter of intent to sell to a prospective buyer

Months 7–8

- Negotiate purchase/sale contract
- Buyer initiates due diligence examination

Month 9

- Lawyers codify purchase agreement and all exhibits
- Buyer completes all due diligence, including closing audit
- Execute contract
- Close

short-term thinking will probably backfire on you. F
not sell your business, you will have to live with
consequences of such moves. Secondly, you should alway
buyers are at least as canny as you are; they will probab
uncover any such financial manoeuvring. When they do,
credibility, and may also lose a deal.

Negotiating and Structuring the Optimal Deal

In the process of building your company, you have undoubtedly spent time at the negotiating table, arranging everything from lease renewals to labour contracts. Yet, in terms of magnitude, time and effort, there is probably very little that will prepare you for the process of negotiating, structuring and closing the sale of your business.

The sale of your business is an all-encompassing matter. Virtually every part of your company will be under scrutiny and will somehow enter into the deal – including the state of your facilities, your management, employees, tax liabilities, pension programmes and out-standing litigation.

Too many owners have consummate faith in their negotiating skills. They enter into negotiations totally unprepared for the enormous task ahead. These owners tend to focus solely on the price they get for their company, leaving the rest of the details to their advisers to work out. Unfortunately, this attitude can lead to very costly mistakes.

Prior to entering into any negotiation to sell your business, you need to define clear and obtainable goals, and then determine a coherent strategy to achieve those goals. You also need to prepare specific data and arguments to quantitatively and analytically support your positions and objectives.

Negotiations are a process of give and take. It is vital that you predetermine what trade-offs you are willing to accept to attain your primary goals.

The two parties to any negotiation generally approach a pending transaction from different perspectives – with completely different, sometimes conflicting, motivations. You, the seller, are looking for the highest price with the fewest possible contingencies. The prospective buyer is seeking the lowest price with the most favourable terms. Depending on your relative bargaining power, one party may have more negotiating leverage than the other – one side may want or need the deal more.

Nevertheless, negotiations tend to lead to successful deals only when both sides approach the talks with an eye toward compromise. Each party needs to believe that he achieved most of his goals, or no deal will ever be consummated. Consequently, each side needs to be willing to accommodate the other.

We generally suggest to our clients that they enter negotiations with an attitude of creating mutually beneficial solutions to impasses or road-blocks. Successfully negotiated deals involve strategic trade-offs. By being flexible and creative, working with your opponent to seek joint solutions to problems, you will probably be able to mould a deal acceptable to both parties.

The right 'chemistry' between a buyer and seller can go a long way toward cementing a deal. You will dramatically increase the probability of a successful deal by working collaboratively with a prospective buyer.

While every negotiation involves unique circumstances, there are a number of universal tips that apply to most situations; here are ten practical tips for successful negotiations.

1. *Keep your eyes on your goals.* Prioritize your objectives up front. Do not get bogged down on unimportant or non-essential issues. Minor points can be addressed after the major issues are resolved. Focus primarily on those goals that are important to you.

2. *Do not expect to win every battle.* You will probably never negotiate a deal if you insist on winning every argument. Negotiations require compromise; you need to let the other side win a few points to get anywhere in negotiations. Indeed, by conceding on some points, you can trade-off to win issues really essential to you. The best deals are so-called 'win-win' situations, where both sides end up getting most of what they want. Just focus on winning those points that are important to you.

3. *Understand the other side's wants and needs.* It is often helpful to put yourself in your opponent's shoes, to understand their reasons for buying your company. Once you see the deal from their vantagepoint, you will be better able to present your goals in a manner acceptable to them.

    If you can determine what is important to the other side and can figure out a way to give them what they want, they should be willing to accommodate you on your points. An example: many buyers are unwilling to take substantial goodwill on to their balance sheets, thus limiting the amount they are willing to pay over your company's stated net worth. Solution: assign some of the consideration above net worth to a non-compete or consulting agreement. This allows the buyer to achieve his goal of minimizing goodwill, while still providing you with the price you seek.

4. *Do not get emotional.* Do not get caught up in the drama of the event, or take matters personally. If you cannot trust yourself to remain calm at negotiations, stay away and let your advisers handle these matters for you.

   You may be surprised how much you can obtain from buyers if you do not reveal your thoughts through your emotions. A client of ours was once hopeful of getting £17 million for his distribution business. He was overjoyed when a prospective buyer threw out an offer of £20 million at the initial negotiating meeting. By maintaining his composure and controlling his emotions, our client was ultimately able to negotiate the buyer up to £22 million.

   Of course, the antithesis occurs as well. Do not be upset or put off by low initial offers. A buyer is only doing his job by trying to buy your company for as little as possible. Do not let your ego either be easily bruised or get in the way of selling your business. Keep calm and stay the course. Negotiations are a process; they take time, patience and a tremendous amount of bargaining.

5. *Be flexible.* The idea of negotiations is to achieve most of your goals through compromise. Always be willing to think of or listen to alternative proposals. As long as you achieve your primary goals, be flexible as to how you get there. There are ways around most log-jams; be creative and work collectively with your opponent to find solutions that work for both parties.

6. *Listen.* Let your opponent do most of the talking. By listening, you draw your opponent out and encourage him to disclose his bargaining position or his ultimate goals. The 'winner' of a negotiation is not the one who controls the conversation, but rather the one who walks away with what he wanted.

7. *Never be afraid to walk away from a deal.* It is important that you never emotionally commit yourself to a buyer until after a deal has been negotiated. Buyers can clearly sense if you want a deal too badly and will naturally take advantage of the situation. To maintain negotiating leverage, you must always be willing to walk away from any deal that does not satisfy your basic requirements. Never put yourself in a position where you feel pressured to take a deal; always leave yourself room to walk. And yet . . .

8. *Never threaten to walk away from a deal unless you mean it.* You only get to walk once. After that, you have lost all credibility and leverage. Walking away from negotiations should only be used as a last resort, not as one of your many negotiating tools.

9. *Deal honestly and openly.* To extract the best deal from a buyer, you must first build an atmosphere of trust. If you have been overtly sly with prospective buyers, or have not been particularly forthcoming, you force buyers to adopt a cautious attitude toward you and your company. You will never achieve a premium deal from a cautious, uncertain buyer.

   Make a policy of cooperating with all prospective buyers. By being honest and open, you will help to make the buyer more comfortable and confident, which will ultimately put him in a position to offer his most attractive deal.

   Many owners feel the need to bluff or lie to achieve their objectives. By creating fictitious offers from ghost buyers, these owners hope to get suitors to bid against themselves. We have rarely seen this ploy work; indeed, the results are generally counter-productive. When uncovered (and they usually are), these ploys will prove embarrassing at best, and could eventually undermine a deal.

10. *Do not over-negotiate.* Stop when you have achieved your goals. Learn to stop when you are ahead. You never know when a buyer is ready to call it quits; by continuing to push and prod, you may quickly find out.

Always maintain a positive negotiating environment. It is a long, arduous road to close a transaction; you want the buyer to be sufficiently motivated to get there. Likewise, to the extent that you remain to run the company, you will end up working closely with your former opponent. If the buyer believed that you acted callously or inappropriately in negotiating the deal, continuing relations with your new owner may be strained.

Negotiations demand considerable patience, which can cause emotional wear and tear on sellers. Recognize that it may take quite a while to finally reach the finish line, and there will be quite a number of hurdles before you get there. Little in life that is worthwhile comes quickly or easily.

Because anxiety may affect your negotiating skills, it is often advisable to have a third party do most of the negotiating for you. This shelters you from most of the daily combat; you participate only when 'broad' agreements have been reached.

Most owners are too close to their businesses to be rational in candidly assessing their situations. Emotions and enthusiasms get the best of all of us. By staying away from the initial stages of negotiations, you are able to maintain a buffer between you and the 'deal'. Allowing a third party to negotiate the early stages of a transaction gives you the upper hand. You get involved only when a pending deal displays sufficient momentum to warrant your participation.

One of our recent clients decided to ignore our advice and got intimately involved in negotiating the sale of his business. He wanted to actively participate in every discussion that related to his company and his deal. As a manufacturer of medical diagnostic equipment, our client's company naturally had some exposure to product liability claims. However, our client's stellar track record and long experience in the field suggested rather minimal exposure to the problem. Indeed, product liability was not initially a major concern to the potential buyer.

None the less, our client was the worrying type. He continually focused discussions on the product liability issue, repeatedly refusing to indemnify against future claims. Our client's anxiety over this point soon made the prospective buyer nervous.

After considerable examination of the matter, the buyer eventually insisted on a large three-year escrow to cover any potential product liability claims. By being too close to the problem, by not seeing the forest for the trees, our client's participation in the negotiations resulted in part of his purchase price being tied up for three years. Had our client not continually harped on the issue, the buyer would undoubtedly have taken a less stringent position on the matter.

Even when negotiating with a sincere, interested buyer, discussions can collapse if a common ground cannot be found. Indeed, you may enter into negotiations with a number of parties, most of which will result in no deal. However friendly or acrimonious the discussions, however far apart you and a buyer are, you should always conclude negotiations on a positive note. Emphasize both the points you agreed on and your continued willingness to resume talks at a later date.

It never pays to burn bridges. You never know how or when the prospective buyer could be useful to you in the future. By leaving the door ajar, you allow both sides the opportunity to re-open negotiations at a later date, should one party or both reconsider their positions.

THE DEAL

The negotiations of a deal do not begin and end with the determination of a purchase price. It is true that the central issue in most negotiations is price. However, matters such as structure, terms, tax treatment of gains, employment agreements, representations and warranties of the seller, and conditions and contingencies on the deal are all integral parts of any deal. These 'peripheral' matters, often overlooked by owners, can have a profound effect on the economics of any deal.

Determining the structure and terms of a transaction can be the most challenging aspect of any deal. Various structures and terms offer abundant opportunities for you to creatively mould a deal to meet your specific needs. Yet, before you enter any negotiation, you need to understand both the differing structures and terms that are available, and their potential ramifications on your deal. Below we provide an overview of the basic deal structures and terms that have evolved over time.

Deal structure

The structure of a transaction refers to the legal and financial form that the deal takes.

Certain structures may be more appropriate than others, depending on your specific liquidity desires, security and diversification goals, and tax strategies. Often, a buyer's circumstances and objectives are at odds with the seller's. You need to understand how your transaction is affected by various structures, and then select the structure that most benefits you. The ultimate structure, of course, will generally be a compromise to balance your needs and wants with those of the buyer.

There are basically four ways to acquire a business; all acquisitions are generally derivatives of one of these four basic forms:

1. A taxable purchase of the stock of a corporation for cash and/or other consideration.

2. A taxable purchase of all or part of the assets of a corporation for cash and/or other consideration.

3. The acquisition of the seller in a tax-deferred exchange for stock of the buyer.

4. The acquisition of all or part of the seller's assets in a tax-deferred exchange of stock.

A stock purchase essentially involves the purchase of a company's capital stock for cash, securities or other consideration. In such a transaction, a buyer purchases the company's balance sheet 'as is', indirectly buying all of the company's assets at their carried (or, in the case of fixed assets, depreciated) value and assuming all of the company's stated and unstated liabilities. The company's tax basis in the assets remains unchanged. The purchaser's tax basis in the stock purchased is equal to the purchase price.

In an asset purchase, an acquirer purchases some or all of a company's assets in exchange for cash, securities, or other property. Concurrent with the purchase, the acquirer assumes some or all of the company's stated liabilities. Typically, an asset purchase includes all of the tangible and intangible assets used in the business, including land and buildings, equipment, inventory, accounts receivable and patents, to name but a few. Once assets are sold, owners of the selling companies often liquidate their companies and distribute all of the proceeds to the shareholders. This structure can give rise to a double tax, once at the corporate level and once at the shareholder level.

Both a stock purchase and an asset purchase contain certain inherent advantages and disadvantages for buyers and sellers alike.

From a buyer's perspective, the main distinction between an asset purchase and a stock purchase is the buyer's tax basis in the acquired assets. In a stock purchase, an acquirer can maintain your company's balance sheet intact. In an asset purchase, however, an acquirer can allocate the purchase price over the various assets acquired. Buyers typically prefer asset deals, primarily because this structure allows them to 'step up' assets to their fair market value. By writing up assets to their fair market value, buyers can minimize the 'goodwill' in a deal.

'Goodwill' is an intangible that reflects the excess over the selling company's net assets that is paid to acquire a business. Goodwill is essentially 'air'; it represents the intangible premium above net worth that an acquirer is willing to pay to buy a company's business and its future earnings stream.

Buyers are often wary of paying too high a premium for a company because of the goodwill they will have to recognize. Because it is amortized over 15 years for tax purposes (20 years in Britain), goodwill can generate a long-term drag on earnings. It also tends to inflate a buyer's balance sheet with too much in the way of intangible assets. Financial analysts and institutional investors tend to penalize companies that have too much goodwill on their balance sheets.

The second major advantage of an asset deal to buyers is that the structure shields an acquirer from any unknown, undisclosed or contingent liabilities. In an asset purchase, a buyer generally assumes only those liabilities that are specifically outlined in the purchase agreement. Indeed, to protect himself, a buyer generally insists upon an express disclaimer and exclusion of all other seller liabilities. Conversely, in a stock deal, a buyer assumes all of the liabilities of your company, whether disclosed or undisclosed, whether on the balance sheet or off. Horror stories abound of acquirers unknowingly buying into undisclosed or unknown litigation or tax liabilities.

Both the ability to 'step up' assets and the concern over hidden liabilities argue strongly for buyers to structure asset deals. However, mitigating factors need to be weighed by buyers: many intangible assets and leases may not be easily assignable. Leases, especially those with 'below market' terms, need to be either renegotiated or assigned in an asset deal, often at significantly increased costs.

In addition, many businesses operate under various contract rights, such as franchises, licences, distribution agreements, or union contracts, most of which are not assignable without consent. A stock purchase leaves these contracts intact, whereas an asset deal will require renegotiation, perhaps resulting in less favourable terms.

Finally, asset deals may require compliance with the bulk sales statutes, which basically require purchasers to notify all seller creditors of the pending transaction to avoid state taxes. Strict compliance with the bulk sales laws is expensive and time-consuming, and can generate unwanted exposure in the marketplace.

As a seller, however, you generally have a different point of view on the matter of a stock purchase versus an asset purchase.

Taxes

In taxable transactions, sellers generally prefer a sale of stock over a sale of assets. An asset sale generally results in double taxation: the selling corporation pays corporate tax when it sells the assets, and the shareholders pay a gains tax when the proceeds are distributed by the corporation to the shareholders.

In the US, S-Corporations, by their very nature, are exempt from this double taxation. Since S-Corporations generally do not pay tax but rather flow their income (and losses) through to their shareholders, double taxation is avoided on the sale of an S-Corporation's assets.

You should be aware, however, that you cannot avoid the double taxation by converting from a C-corporation to an S-Corporation immediately prior to a sale. In such instances, the tax law imposes a corporate tax on the 'built-in gain' in your company's assets as of the time of the conversion to an S-Corporation.

Cost

An asset deal is generally more complex, expensive and time-consuming than a stock deal. An asset transaction requires a legal transfer of each asset, often triggering a variety of taxes. In addition, it can be a long and costly endeavour to renegotiate or obtain consents to assign leases, licences or other contract rights. A stock sale, on the other hand, merely requires transfer of stock certificates, generally a far simpler transaction, resulting in much lower legal fees.

Liabilities

In an asset deal, a buyer specifically limits his assumption of liabilities to those outlined in the purchase agreement. However, in a stock deal, the buyer directly assumes all corporate liabilities, including contingent and unknown liabilities. However, you should be aware that even in a stock deal, you will be called on to list all known company liabilities and indemnify a buyer against any undisclosed liabilities. Thus, a stock deal is not as advantageous as it appears; you will generally still remain exposed for contingent or undisclosed liabilities relating to events that occurred in your company up until the closing.

Deal terms

Price and terms are intimately intertwined; one is generally very dependent on the other. An integral part of the price of a deal is the terms under which the price is paid. There is an often-used phrase in the merger business: 'You name the price, and I'll name the terms.' Clearly, there is a significant difference between a deal for £25 million in cash and a deal for £25 million in a 5 per cent, 20-year balloon note. Owners who focus on maximizing price in such a cavalier manner without regard to terms generally wind up only fooling themselves.

Alternatively, some owners approach the sale of their company with only one acceptable term in mind: cash. A cash deal is certainly the cleanest method of payment; it also offers the least risk. However, a cash transaction may not be the most logical way to fulfil your liquidity objectives. Alternative methods will allow you to spread-out, defer or possibly eliminate a taxable gain. Other terms will allow you to continue to share in the growth or profitability of your company. Lastly, you may find that by being flexible, you can get a significantly better overall deal than would be possible with an all-cash transaction. Sometimes, regardless of your preferences, the only way that you will ever get a buyer to pay your price is by being flexible on the terms.

In reality, most sales of private, middle-market companies are not all-cash deals. Most deals involve varying combinations of cash, stock, notes, non-compete payments, consulting/employment agreements, royalties or contingent 'earn-outs'. At times, a buyer cannot fund all of the purchase price in cash and needs you to finance part of the deal.

Alternatively, a buyer may want part of the purchase price to be in the form of a deductible employment agreement or non-compete payment, to provide him with some tax relief.

The key to negotiating the optimal deal is to decide at the outset what price and what terms will be acceptable to you. Remember that there is generally a very tight interplay between price and terms; flexibility or rigidity in one generally affects the other. With that in mind, below is a brief elaboration of the most common terms you will encounter.

Promissory notes

Buyers generally ask sellers to take back promissory notes either to help finance part of the purchase price, or because the buyers do not want to finance the transaction themselves in the commercial markets. Notes offer many opportunities to creatively balance buyers' and sellers' interests, especially in the areas of security, amortization and interest.

One way to structure a mutually acceptable note is to evaluate various amortization options, including 'interest only' periods and 'balloon' payments, as alternatives to equal instalments of interest and principal. By agreeing to a ten-year amortization on your five-year note, say, you provide the buyer with some initial repayment relief in exchange for a shorter maturity than he might normally offer.

With regard to appropriate interest rates, it is important to remember that whatever notes you take back must bear interest of at least the rate the Treasury pays for obligations of similar maturity (referred to as 'the applicable Federal rate'). If the stated interest is at a lower rate, or there is no stated interest, then the tax authorities will 'impute' a tax on the difference (the interest the tax man says you should have received). The thinking here is that it is not a prudent investment to take back $15 million (£10 million) in a 5 per cent note when government bonds of a similar maturity are yielding 8 per cent. Thus, the tax authorities assume that part of the $15 million (£10 million) is actually 'hidden' interest, and make you pay an annual tax on that interest.

Many owners actually prefer to include notes as an integral element of their deal. A note offers one significant advantage over cash – the opportunity to postpone the tax on that portion of the purchase price that is represented by the note. By taking part of the purchase price in a note and electing an 'instalment sale', you can postpone the recognition of your gain, thus allowing you to spread your tax liabilities pro rata over the term of the note. The 'instalment sale' option can be very attractive to sellers who have a need or desire to defer their tax liability.

Consulting/employment agreements

There are very legitimate reasons for buyers to pay owners for continued consulting or employment: to compensate them for vital services rendered. However, payments for consulting or employment also offer fertile ground for buyers to pay you additional money for your business while providing them with some tax relief.

By offering consulting agreements with few obligations attached, or inflating compensation in an employment agreement, buyers are able to funnel more money to a seller, in effect increasing the purchase price. This is attractive to acquirers because employment payments are deductible, thus providing buyers with some tax benefits. All consideration that is paid for your stock or assets comes from after-tax money. Employment or consulting payments come from pre-tax money.

In addition, buyers tend to want to attach part of the purchase price to a consulting/employment agreement to help minimize the goodwill in a deal. As deductible, on-going expenses, these agreements rarely make it on to a balance sheet. If they do, they are amortized far quicker than goodwill.

Payments for covenants not to compete ('non-compete payments')

It is customary for all purchase agreements to include a 'covenant not to compete' – in effect, a clause preventing owners from directly or indirectly competing with their companies once they have sold. Most buyers will insist on some form of non-compete. After all, a company's most important asset is its people. A buyer's worst nightmare is that he buys you out, only to have you go across the street to establish a competing business.

A non-compete covenant ostensibly enhances the value of your business. Therefore, many acquirers allocate a part of the purchase price to the non-compete, and want to pay you a separate consideration for that covenant. Generally, a non-compete is amortized over the length of its life (typically 3–5 years). Buyers tend to want the non-compete payments to mirror this amortization schedule.

The benefits of non-compete payments for buyers are essentially the same as with consulting/employment payments: they can be tax-deductible and can help to eliminate goodwill from a deal. In addition, by attaching some of the purchase price to a non-compete payment, buyers give their non-compete covenants some teeth in the eyes of the courts. After all, they not only paid you for your business, they also gave you a separate and distinct payment not to compete.

Contingent payments/earn-outs

Earn-outs are generally a way to resolve differences of opinion over the value of a company by basing part of the purchase price on the future performance of the company.

Sellers are typically very optimistic about future prospects; buyers tend to be more conservative. An earn-out is a mechanism to acknowledge the seller's optimism towards the future, but to compensate such optimism only if and when the results are realized. A seller gains some assurance that the ultimate purchase price fairly reflects the future earnings potential, while the purchaser guards against paying too much for a company.

Earn-outs tend to be based on the future operating performance of the selling company. Typical earn-outs provide for additional payments to a seller if earnings exceed agreed-upon levels, or a sharing of earnings over a pre-set time frame. Two differing examples: an earn-out that provides for 5 per cent of sales over a five-year period versus one that allows for 15 per cent of operating profit until £3 million is earned. The structure generally depends on the motivations and the concerns of the buyer.

Contingent earn-outs make the most sense when an owner is staying on to run his company after the sale. The owner can thus have a direct impact on his company's performance and therefore his future payments. Buyers often use earn-outs as a way to continue to provide incentives to sellers who otherwise would have no economic interest in the companies they continue to operate. Earn-outs provide sellers with an opportunity to continue to participate in the growth and profitability of their companies.

Payments can take many forms: they can be structured as royalties, as bonuses, or as part of the consideration paid for the business. If an earn-out is paid as part of the consideration for the business, it can qualify as an instalment sale, with a tax liability only if and when earned. Obviously, most acquirers would prefer to structure contingent payments as bonuses or royalties, as these payments are deductible expenses.

While attractive in theory, earn-outs can be difficult to administer in practice. From the start, both parties need to agree on definitions of certain key terms used to calculate the contingent payment, like 'earnings', 'profits', or 'net income'. Also, to fairly determine earnings, a purchaser should agree to operate the business as a separate entity, consistent with past practice (including maintenance of accounting standards). Obviously, it is difficult to gauge the performance of an acquired company if it is combined with or merged into the buyer's operation.

Sellers should also clarify how corporate administrative charges or inter-company transactions may affect their ability to reach the earn-out goals. Issues such as depreciation, non-recurring expenses and on-going capital expenditures also need to be addressed.

In the end, no legal document can fully protect both parties in an earn-out. There are an infinite number of administrative problems to work out, most of which can never be fully or properly addressed in a contract. For earn-outs to work, both buyer and seller must ultimately have an implicit, 'good faith' trust in one another.

Because of the contingent nature of earn-outs, we generally advise clients that they should be reasonably content with all of the other aspects of their deal, as if those aspects were the only consideration they will receive. Before accepting an earn-out, you should recognize that you may earn nothing from the earn-out, that forces beyond your control may deny you any future payments. Therefore, you must be satisfied with the initial 'down payment' as compensation for your company. Any earn-out payments, if and when they come, are 'gravy'.

Stock

Except in tax-deferred transactions (discussed in the 'Tax Consider-ations' section of this chapter), stock is generally an unattractive method of payment for your company. In any taxable transaction, sellers who receive part of the purchase price in stock are liable for the full tax liability on the fair market value of that stock. Since the government will not accept stock to satisfy the tax liability, and since most stock conveyed in an acquisition has some trading restrictions, you will have to use a disproportionate amount of the cash portion of your deal to cover the liability associated with the stock. Because of this, most deals utilizing stock fall into one of the tax-deferred acquisition categories discussed later.

If you are enamoured with the prospects of the stock of your prospective acquirer, it makes more economic sense to just use some of your cash proceeds to buy the stock in the open market. On the other hand, some buyers insist on using their own stock as currency.

If you are considering taking stock, you should investigate whether the shares will be registered or unregistered (that is, whether they are able to be freely traded or not). Even if they are registered, you need to further examine what restrictions, if any, apply to the shares.

Tax considerations

Taxes are a very real and often unavoidable cost of selling your business. Most acquisitions are taxable transactions; that is, any gain realized from the sale (the gross proceeds less the adjusted basis) is taxable. It is important that you fully understand the tax treatment and cost of any proposed transaction. Taxes, or the deferral of them, can have a dramatic impact on the economics of your deal.

Taxes are probably the prime consideration of both buyers and sellers in selecting an appropriate structure for a deal. Buyers, of course, try to minimize the tax costs of buying a company. Sellers, on the other hand, attempt to maximize their net after-tax proceeds. The eventual structure is generally a compromise between these two differing, often conflicting, motivations. It is possible, however, to structure some transactions so that they are either totally tax-deferred or partially tax-deferred to the seller.

A taxable deal generally results from the acquisition of a selling company's stock or assets through the use of cash, notes or other consideration. On the other hand, tax-deferred deals are generally effected by the 'purchasing' company exchanging stock for the assets or stock of the 'selling' company, where the 'sellers' have a continuing, direct equity participation in the combined entity. Partially taxable deals are essentially a combination of the two, accomplished through an exchange of both stock and cash (or other consideration).

The concept behind a tax-deferred transaction is that a seller has not really sold his company. Rather, he merely combined it with another company, thus not triggering a taxable transaction. Instances where sellers receive cash, notes or the like are considered taxable because the stock or the assets of the companies are indeed being sold for tangible consideration.

To qualify as 'tax-deferred', a transaction must meet a number of litmus tests, including conditions on the structure and payments of the acquisition.

Sellers are often attracted to tax-deferred acquisitions for one main reason: the gain on the sale is not recognized for tax purposes. Rather, a seller incurs a tax on the stock only if and when it is subsequently sold in the open market, and then only to the extent of the stock sold. (Tax-deferred transactions can indeed be truly 'tax free' for sellers, but only if they die retaining the stock. In such an instance, your estate and beneficiaries can 'step up' the value of the stock to its fair market value, thus eliminating the built-in gain and the capital gains tax.)

Buyers are attracted to tax-deferred transactions for one of three primary reasons: 1) to accommodate a seller's concerns over the tax liability generated by a deal; 2) to preserve cash; or 3) to maintain the seller's tax basis in the stock or assets that are acquired. Through an exchange of stock and the concurrent election of the 'pooling of interests' method of accounting, a buyer can simply assume the historic basis in the selling company's stock or assets, thus avoiding burdensome goodwill.

A 'pooling of interests' assumes a merger of two entities into one, as though the new, combined entity always existed. The assets and liabilities of both companies are carried at their historic costs. This can be quite attractive for buyers in transactions that involve purchase prices well in excess of the book value of the stock or assets being acquired. Buyers can effectively avoid the entire issue of assuming goodwill.

Tax-deferred transactions typically fall into one of three categories:

- a statutory merger;
- an exchange of stock for stock;
- an exchange of assets for stock.

Various hybrids and permutations exist, but all are variations of these three basic forms.

In a *statutory merger*, one corporation completely absorbs another; it is a continuation of two (or more) companies assembled into one new corporation. All shareholders of the previous companies become shareholders in the new company. Such mergers are generally governed by legal statutes (thus the name). A statutory merger is often considered the most flexible of the three tax-deferred structures available.

To maintain sufficient continuing equity interest in the continuing company and, thus, to qualify for tax-deferred status, at least 50 per cent of the purchase price in a statutory merger must be paid in the acquiring company's stock (voting or non-voting). This means that up to 50 per cent of the purchase price can be paid in cash or other consideration (of course, a tax liability is triggered on all consideration that is received other than stock).

In a *stock-for-stock acquisition*, the 'buying' company acquires the 'selling' company's stock solely in exchange for its voting stock. The payment for the shares is limited to voting stock; no other form of consideration is allowed, lest the entire transaction be deemed taxable. Accordingly, a stock-for-stock exchange is considered the simplest but most restrictive form of tax-free transaction.

A *stock for assets transaction* involves a deal whereby the acquiring company purchases 'substantially all' of the selling company's assets in exchange for voting stock. Because of their complexity, 'stock for asset' deals are very rare.

The main attractiveness of tax-deferred deals to sellers is that such transactions allow owners to exchange their illiquid and untraded holdings in their private companies for stock that is both freely traded and has some growth potential. Such a transaction provides owners with an opportunity to get some liquidity for their shares, while incurring a tax liability only if, when and to the extent that the stock is sold.

However, a tax-deferred deal may be totally inappropriate for you, especially if your personal objectives are to gain instant liquidity and to bring some diversity to your assets. There are customary restrictions on the after-market selling of any stock you receive in a stock swap. Additionally, it is often difficult to quickly and efficiently liquefy a major position in a stock. As for diversity, a stock swap merely exchanges all of the stock in your private company for stock in that of the acquirer. Your entire holdings benefit with the appreciation of the acquirer's stock, but they also suffer with any decline.

Summary

As should be obvious in reading this chapter, there are many complex legal, accounting, regulatory and tax issues involved in negotiating and structuring a deal. Differing deal structures offer differing tax ramifications. On top of that, tax laws and accounting standards are constantly changing.

A prudent business owner will recognize the limits of his knowledge of these areas and will engage expert advisers to help guide him through the maze. The information in this book is cursory in its coverage of the important legal, accounting and tax aspects of acquisitions. It cannot serve as a substitute for professional advice.

Many business owners naturally turn to their long-time corporate accountants and lawyers for such advice. Because of their intimate knowledge of both the selling company and the personal affairs of the owner, these professionals are often the correct choice. However, many accountants and lawyers who are perfectly capable of handling routine corporate affairs are totally incapable of handling the many complex aspects of an acquisition. The area of mergers and acquisitions is considered a speciality; those professionals with specific experience in this area generally have an advantage over those who do not. Experienced professionals pay for themselves many times over, not only for what they advise you to do, but also for what they advise you not to do.

If a corporate acquirer is coming to a negotiating table with a major law or accounting firm advising him, you need to match him with equivalent experience and ability. After all, you do not want your accountant and legal adviser learning on your deal. Thus it may behove you to seek a different set of professionals to arrange the sale of your company than your customary corporate advisers.

As a side issue, you should always be aware of the inherent conflict of interest in retaining your customary advisers. After all, your company is probably a major account to both your law and accounting firms. Naturally, these professionals will be concerned about losing your business after the deal is done.

We have witnessed numerous instances where the lawyers or accountants did not act in the best interests of their client, seeking to undermine a deal to rescue their on-going account. One of the most egregious instances was when the accountant of a Chicago-based client both purposely lost certain key business records and continually brought negative aspects of the business to the prospective buyer's attention. Unfortunately, both we and our client were totally unaware of the accountant's shenanigans until after the deal died.

Even without obvious duplicity, there is a natural, unavoidable conflict that cannot help but colour the relationship between you and your professionals. By hiring outsiders, you totally eliminate this problem.

If you do decide to retain your regular professionals, you might consider offering a generous severance payment, contingent on the deal closing, in order to align their interests with yours. It is always important to keep your professionals oriented toward the deal. After all, once you have made a decision to sell, you want everyone on your team focused on your goals.

THE LETTER OF INTENT

Once two parties reach an agreement in principal as to the basic price, structure and terms of a transaction, they typically enter into what is termed a 'letter of intent' (also referred to as 'heads of agreement'.) The letter of intent is a written outline of the general agreements between buyer and seller, serving to clarify and crystallize in writing the basic terms of the deal. A letter of intent can be viewed as a marker on the road to a completed deal; both sides stop by the side to codify in writing the basic agreements that have been reached thus far in the process.

Typically drafted as a letter from the buyer to the seller, a letter of intent generally sets out the proposed price, terms and structure of a transaction, as well as the conditions and contingencies on closing the deal.

In most instances, a letter of intent does not create a binding obligation; rather, it spells out the 'intent' of both parties to close the transaction along the lines of the terms presented. However, letters of intent generally do create binding obligations on each side to continue to maintain confidentiality and to bear their own legal and accounting expenses.

Most letters of intent also contain a binding 'no-shop clause', which basically prohibits your courting other suitors or negotiating with other parties for a specified time frame (generally 45–90 days). Most buyers will insist on a 'no-shop' clause, primarily to allow themselves sufficient time to complete their detailed examination of your company and to negotiate and execute a binding purchase agreement. Buyers have to expend considerable time, effort and expense in completing a deal; they naturally only want to proceed if they can get a like commitment out of you. If you are serious about a specific buyer and a specific deal, you should be willing to provide this 'exclusive' window of time.

There are two main advantages for a seller to enter into a letter of intent:

1. It clearly and succinctly outlines the basic terms of deal for all parties to witness. A letter of intent provides written proof of mutually agreed terms and conditions, should either party attempt to change the deal or re-negotiate later on.

2. You obtain a moral, if not legal, commitment from a buyer to use his good faith efforts to close on the transaction outlined in the letter. (Incidentally, you also get an indirect financial commitment, in that a letter of intent will cost the buyer significant legal fees to draft.)

Though each letter of intent is unique in reflecting the specific circumstances of each transaction, most cover the following issues:

- *The price and terms of the deal.* The price may be expressed as a fixed number or as a formula (often expressed as the selling company's net worth, plus or minus a fixed amount, with the net worth to be determined as of the day of close). There is generally a clause to cover what happens to the company's earnings between the execution of the letter of intent and the closing, and how those earnings are to be paid out. There should also be a full description of the terms and restrictions of any notes or securities to be conveyed.

- *The structure of the deal.* This section should address whether the transaction is structured as purchase of stock or assets, or a statutory merger, and should include descriptions of special accounting or tax considerations inherent in the proposed structure.
- *The time frame for negotiating the purchase agreement.* Generally 45–90 days, during which time most acquirers demand a no-shop clause. Most letters of intent self-terminate at the end of the period.
- *The specifics of any employment agreements, consulting agreements or covenants not-to-compete.* Issues surrounding employment and consulting agreements include the term, compensation and specific duties to be performed. Non-compete covenants need to be defined in terms of activity, time and place.
- *The conditions and contingencies of the deal.* A listing of the conditions and contingencies that must be met prior to a close, such as financing for the deal, a complete audit of your company's books, or regulatory approvals. If one of the conditions is a full examination of your company, the procedures and time frame under which that examination takes place should be clearly defined.

Examples of two 'typical' letters of intent, one short and one more detailed, are provided in Appendix II.

Because the letter of intent may include some legally binding clauses, it is not advisable for you to enter into one without first consulting your legal adviser.

Unlike many property deals, most transactions involving companies do not include 'binders' or 'earnest money'. A prospective buyer of your company makes an offer based on very cursory data, almost all of it supplied by you. Thus, in making an offer, the buyer has assumed that all of the information you have provided is accurate and complete. It is rare that buyers will pay 'earnest money' on an offer which is based on totally unverified information.

Instead, prior to entering into a letter of intent with a suitor, do your homework on your prospective acquirer. Convince yourself of their ability to finance the acquisition of your company. Review their history of prior acquisitions: examine both their record of closing deals and their record of success with those companies after acquisition. Diligent examination of the prospective buyer will provide a much higher degree of comfort than any 'earnest money'. After all, you are not going through this process merely to pocket some 'earnest money'; you are seeking to sell your company.

Lastly, you should not equate the execution of a letter of intent with the closing of a deal. A letter of intent is but one step, albeit an important one, on the road to a deal. Much can happen to derail your deal between the letter of intent and the closing. For this reason, we generally suggest that owners do not reveal the letter of intent or the proposed deal to customers, suppliers or employees (except on a 'need to know' basis). There will be plenty of time for jubilation once you have cemented the deal.

The Purchase Agreement and Closing the Deal

There is an old saying in the merger business: ' A deal is never done until you have received the cheque . . . and it has cleared.' How true that is! The entire acquisition process is dynamic, constantly in flux until the day of a closing. To borrow from Yogi Berra, a deal is never over until it's over.

Once you have negotiated a price, structure and terms, and have then codified your agreement in a letter of intent, you are on the home stretch. But you cannot give up the race at this point. You still have two vital legs to run before the race is over: presiding over the buyer's due diligence process and negotiating and executing the purchase agreement. The two processes generally occur simultaneously, primarily because it is in everyone's best interest to close on an agreed deal as soon as possible.

Unlike wine, deals do not age well; they tend to get stale with time. The longer it takes to close a deal, the more time buyers have to rethink or renege on their obligations. As time drags on, there is also an increasing likelihood that word will leak out. Time generally hurts sellers more than buyers, especially with regard to customers or employees, so remain diligent about pushing your deal along.

Once a letter of intent is executed, it is customary for both sides to agree to a 45–90 day time frame to complete a deal. You can always extend the period if need be, but it is important for you to keep the time pressure on the buyer (as well as your accountants and legal advisers), lest nothing will proceed as scheduled.

You should also remember that even though you have generally agreed to a deal, negotiations are never over until a deal closes. You still have to go through the process of producing a mutually acceptable purchase agreement, which involves its own set of negotiations. In addition, there are certain buyers who will wait until the day of the closing before attempting to renegotiate a deal, counting on easy capitulation from sellers already committed to a deal. Of course, you should never be overly suspicious or cautious. Still, you should remain diligent throughout the process and never let your guard down.

DUE DILIGENCE

Buyers generally make offers on your business based solely on information provided by you. Until the letter of intent has been executed, buyers have no opportunity to either verify that the information provided to them was accurate and complete, or to otherwise engage in a diligent and thorough examination of the business that they are about to buy.

The term 'due diligence' has its genesis in the US Securities Act of 1933, which basically outlined methods to achieve 'full and fair disclosure' of all pertinent material facts relating to publicly held securities. The Act provided a general overview of the breadth and depth of information that companies must provide to investors so that those parties can engage in proper 'due diligence' prior to investing. In the market for private companies, 'due diligence' has come to refer to the process by which a prospective buyer both verifies all previously provided data and also undertakes a full review of all other relevant information prior to legally committing to a deal. While corporate raiders may initiate take-overs of large public companies without proper due diligence, it is rare that anyone will buy a smaller private company without a thorough examination of all aspects of the company before committing any money.

While each buyer will want to examine differing aspects of your business in differing degrees of detail, due diligence inquiries generally focus on the following broad areas:

- corporate organization and ownership;
- products, including the manufacturing process and markets;
- customers and suppliers;
- sales and marketing;
- facilities and equipment;
- management and employees;
- reporting and control systems;
- financial results and balance sheet.

A detailed listing of a typical 'due diligence checklist' is provided in Appendix III.

More likely than not, a buyer will engage his legal adviser to conduct a thorough study of your company' s corporate documents and legal standing. A buyer will also probably engage his accounting firm to perform a full financial audit, both to produce a closing balance sheet and to verify all past financial records.

While much of a buyer' s due diligence can take place at your accountant's or legal adviser's office, it will be necessary for the buyer to conduct some of his examination at your facilities. A buyer will certainly want the opportunity to fully inspect your physical plant. In addition, they will want to meet and interview your company's management, to get comfortable with both their operating abilities and their future commitment to the company.

It is unreasonable to deny access to your facilities or management during a due diligence period; on the other hand, by no means should a prospective buyer have open access to your company. The letter of intent should outline in detail all due diligence procedures, which generally require that all plant visits and management interviews be arranged through you. It is customary that all due diligence occurs during business hours. To minimize exposure, however, you may want to arrange for some due diligence visits to occur after hours.

Due diligence is a necessary evil in getting a deal done. The process will become very tedious very quickly. You will undoubtedly tire of the endless requests for information or explanations of company practices. Very little of your past or present operations will go uncovered or unnoticed. And yet, throughout the process, you need to keep in mind that you would probably go into just as much painful detail if you were buying your own company. After all, you have had years to understand the internal workings of your company; a prospective buyer has at best a few months to acquaint himself. You need to have the patience to educate your buyer as to all the mundane but vital details of your company.

THE PURCHASE AGREEMENT

A purchase agreement is a legal document which sets forth all of the agreements and understandings between the buyer and seller of a business. The purchase document not only covers the price, terms and structure of a deal, but it also details all of the other legal and financial aspects of the transaction. Unlike a letter of intent, an acquisition agreement is legally binding; a party to the agreement that fails to perform is liable for damages.

As with the letter of intent, it is customarily the buyer's respons-ibility to draft the purchase agreement. While this may appear unfair, there is a certain logic to it. A purchase agreement is basically written for the protection of the buyer. After all, a seller walks away from a deal with cash. The buyer' s only source of recourse for fraud or misrepresentation is the purchase agreement.

None the less, the drafting of the purchase agreement constitutes an enormous advantage for the buyer; he not only gets to frame the initial document to favour his interests, but he also has the opportunity to add points or conditions not previously negotiated.

We have never been involved with a purchase agreement that has not undergone several rounds of substantial redrafting before a mutually acceptable document is produced.

The negotiation of the purchase document essentially picks up where the negotiations of the letter of intent left off. Copies of the tables of contents of two purchase agreements, one for an asset deal and one for a stock deal, are provided in Appendix IV. In general, most acquisition agreements cover the following areas.

The price, terms and structure of the deal

Most purchase agreements commence with what is generally con-sidered the most important feature of the document: a detailed description of the price, terms and structure of the transaction.

The first issue to be addressed is generally the structure of the deal: whether the deal will take the form of a stock transaction, an asset transaction, a recapitalization or a merger. In the case of an asset transaction, the document must include a full accounting of exactly what assets are being sold; what assets, if any, are being excluded; and what specific liabilities are being assumed by the buyer.

The price is generally expressed as either a fixed amount (say '£16 million') or a formula ('the selling company's net worth plus $10 million'). Typically, formulas are used when the purchase price is pegged to the selling company' s balance sheet as of the closing date. The deal is closed based on an estimated balance sheet, with post-closing adjustments made after the preparation of a final closing balance sheet.

This section of the document also identifies and explains in detail all of the terms that constitute the purchase price, including cash, notes, stock or contingent payments.

Representations and warranties

Representations and warranties refer to binding claims each party makes with respect to their company and the transaction. In this section of the purchase agreement, both the buyer and the seller warrant certain claims to each other.

Buyers' representations are generally limited to the fact that they are legally and financially able to make the acquisition.

Sellers' representations are generally much broader and far-reaching. Most sellers are called on to make detailed representations and warranties as to the nature and condition of their companies, in addition to their legal ability to consummate the transaction.

Questions over the nature and extent of seller representations are generally the most fertile ground for argument and negotiations between a buyer and a seller. After paying a fair price for a business, a buyer naturally wants some assurances as to the legal, financial and business aspects of the selling company. Almost without question, buyers will demand to be protected from contingent, undisclosed or unknown liabilities, such as outstanding litigation, environmental problems or unpaid taxes. Buyers logically argue that such liabilities may detract from the value of the business – had they been aware of such liabilities at the outset, they would have offered a commensurably lower amount. Thus, buyers want a mechanism to be compensated for any undisclosed or unknown liabilities that existed at the time of the closing. (This is not to be confused with buyers wanting protection from ordinary business risk. No one expects sellers to warrant against business failure caused by inept management, competition, a loss of customers, or a downturn in the economy.)

Representations and warranties are intended to set forth both parties' mutual understanding of the selling company. Through this exercise, buyers will ostensibly have a full understanding and assurance as to what they are buying.

Most sellers attempt to sell their companies 'as is' , shunning any on-going exposure in the future. However, rarely will a buyer proceed on a transaction where he cannot get a minimum of representations and warranties from a seller.

It is typical for sellers to at least warrant the following:

- The selling corporation is in good standing and has good and marketable title to all assets and properties. The company has all required licences and permits to conduct its business and is not in violation of any regulatory codes.
- All contract rights and leases are in good standing and not in threat of being terminated.

- No litigation exists or is pending against the company (except as specified).
- There are no liens or encumbrances on any of the company assets (except as specified).
- All financial statements fairly and accurately present the company's financial condition and recent performance.
- All required tax returns have been filed, and all tax payments are current.
- There are no liabilities other than those that the seller has detailed in the various schedules and exhibits of the purchase agreement.

Since you know the most about your company, you are the one who should be in the best position to understand the risks associated with each of the representations and warranties demanded by a buyer. Your refusal to provide a specific warranty may cause buyers to become wary.

Still, it is to your advantage to eliminate or very narrowly define the warranties you have to make regarding your company. The fewer and more specific the representations and warranties, the less exposure you have to claims for damages after the closing.

Covenants

The closing of a deal often occurs simultaneously with the execution of the purchase agreement. However, for a number of reasons, closing can occur after the actual signing of the agreement.

Buyers may want to quickly sign an agreement for specific tax or accounting reasons, leaving the fine details of actually closing the deal to a later date. Alternatively, many banks will commit to lend money for a deal only after an agreement has been fully executed by both sides. The covenants section of the purchase document outlines the obligations of each party during the period between the signing and the closing.

While some covenants pertain to the buyer's conduct during this period (such as the maintenance of confidentiality), most are directed at the seller. These covenants protect the buyer from major changes in the legal, financial or business aspects of the selling company pending the closing.

Sellers are generally obliged to carry on in the normal course of business, undertaking no new projects and incurring no new indebtedness or extraordinary expenditures, including bonuses or dividends. Indeed, most covenants are aimed at maintaining the status quo at the selling company.

The logic behind these covenants is obvious: once you have agreed to sell the stock of your company for £10 million, a buyer wants to protect against you pulling a £2 million dividend out of the company just before closing, making the de facto cost to the buyer grow to £12 million.

Covenants can be either affirmative or negative; that is, they can either demand that you do something (like maintain a certain net worth) or not do something (like take a dividend). Negative covenants are termed such because they prohibit sellers from acts that would diminish the value of the business.

If a seller is receiving a separate payment not to compete, there will typically be a separate non-compete document. Otherwise, covenants not to compete will also be covered in this section of the purchase document.

Most buyers will insist on some form of non-compete as a part of the overall agreement. As discussed earlier, a covenant not to compete essentially prevents owners from directly or indirectly competing with their companies once they have sold. In any deal, an acquirer is ostensibly buying both your tangible assets and your intangible assets – such as your way of doing business, your customer relationships and your technical or marketing know-how. Naturally, a buyer will want a mechanism to prevent competitors from getting those intangibles.

Courts have displayed a willingness to enforce the restrictions of non-compete covenants as a part of the sale of a business, especially where separate and distinct payments were attached to those covenants. And yet, courts traditionally recognize only those non-compete covenants that are specific in terms of prohibited activities, duration and geography. It would be unreasonable to deny you the opportunity to ever work again in the textile business in the UK, for instance. However, a non-compete preventing you from competing in the men's apparel field within a 100 mile radius of London for five years would most probably be enforceable.

Precedence generally dictates that non-compete covenants are enforceable for a 3–5 year time frame; anything beyond that is generally considered unreasonable.

Most buyers will want to define the covenant as broadly as their legal counsel will allow. You should certainly attempt to narrow the agreement to a workable arrangement. However, we have seen too many owners expend great time and effort in negotiating limitations on the non-compete, often causing quite a commotion in the process. If you sincerely have no intention of ever competing, or are selling to retire from business, it is far preferable to concede to a broadly defined non-compete in exchange for other points that are more important to you.

Conditions to the closing

If the signing and the closing do not occur simultaneously, most purchase agreements include a section outlining the conditions precedent to the closing. This section lists conditions under which either the buyer or the seller have the right to terminate the agreement without being liable for damages. If all of these conditions are met, then both parties are obligated to close. Of course, even if certain conditions are not met, both sides can mutually agree to proceed with the deal anyway.

Typical conditions to a deal are the clearance of the transaction by regulatory agencies, the satisfactory financing of the deal, or the transference of a lease. In addition, buyers will want to make certain that you are in conformity with all of the affirmative and negative covenants before closing.

Because the conditions to a closing typically benefit the buyer, you need to make certain that all conditions are reasonable and specific. Before you sign any 'conditional' agreement, you must soberly assess the sincerity and ability of the buyer to close the transaction. The last thing that you want is to be bound by an open-ended, conditional agreement, which amounts to giving the buyer an 'option' on your company. After all, the seller generally has little control over many of the conditions, such as the buyer securing satisfactory financing.

Often, conditional agreements are unavoidable. Many banks will consider giving final approval to finance a deal only after the seller has already signed a definitive agreement. Still, you should very narrowly specify both the number and the breadth of any conditions, in addition to imposing a strict deadline for the buyer to satisfy those conditions.

Indemnification

The indemnification section of the purchase agreement establishes the liability of each party for problems that are discovered after the closing. This section essentially outlines the circumstances and procedures under which either party can claim damages in the event of a breach of the representations or warranties.

As with most other sections of the purchase document, the indemnification section is primarily for the protection of the buyer. Buyers will generally insist that you indemnify them for problems that arise from a breach of representations and warranties after the close. This is only fair. After all, an acquirer will buy your company based on certain representations. If things are not as you portrayed them, buyers understandably want some recourse.

While a buyer would probably be able to take legal action against a seller in the event of fraud or misrepresentation anyway, the indemnification section clearly and succinctly defines the procedures under which a buyer can come after you to recover damages.

Of course, this section typically contains cross-indemnification; the buyer agrees to indemnify you in the event of a breach of his representations and warranties, however slight that possibility is.

The duration of an indemnity is generally a major point of contention. Without a specific provision setting a time frame, it is possible that the representations and warranties may not 'survive' past the closing. However, most buyers insist on at least a 1–2 year 'window' during which sellers are fully liable for all breaches.

Another issue to address with regard to seller indemnification is the total aggregate amount of exposure a seller has to buyer claims. Courts have often found that, except in instances of fraud or misrepresentation, sellers generally cannot be liable for any more than the full purchase price they received in the transaction. Frankly, because most major issues are uncovered in due diligence, we have found buyers willing to limit seller exposure to a fraction of the purchase price (generally in the range of 50 per cent). This gives the sellers some comfort that not all the consideration is 'at risk', and yet still provides a buyer with the knowledge that significant funds are available for unforeseen breaches or problems.

Rarely do transactions involving private companies not eventually produce some breaches of warranties. From the uncollectability of some receivables to a contractual commitment gone sour, it is almost a certainty that some problems will arise during the 'survival' period.

Sellers have a legitimate concern about being held accountable for a series of small, picayune claims by the buyer. Thus it is customary for both parties to establish a mechanism where sellers are only liable for claims based on significant problems, or where minor breaches aggregate to significant problems.

The typical solution to this dilemma is to establish a 'basket'. A basket is a minimum threshold which must be reached, singularly or in the aggregate, before a seller's liability is triggered. By establishing a basket, a buyer cannot seek to recover damages unless and until total claims meet a certain, pre-set aggregate amount. A basket shields a seller from dealing with innumerable petty claims, while at the same time protecting the buyer from suffering egregious damages.

Baskets typically range from 1 to 2 per cent of the total purchase price, or, say, $200 000 (£125 000) on a $20 million (£12.5 million) transaction. Baskets generally work in one of two ways: either the seller is liable for the entire amount of the damages once the basket has been 'tipped', or he is liable for only those claims above the basket threshold. (In other words, in a situation with a £200 000 basket and £400 000 of claims, the first scenario would leave the seller liable for the full £400 000, while the second scenario would limit his exposure to only the excess £200 000.) Of course, the mechanism and threshold of the basket is subject to negotiation. Expect buyers to initially refuse to even consider a basket, though most end up capitulating to the notion.

No buyer wants to face the unenviable task of attempting to retrieve a part of the purchase price from a seller. This becomes especially difficult when the seller was paid in cash and has either squandered the money or has moved to some far-away country. To protect their interests and make certain that there will be adequate funds available to satisfy their claims, most buyers will insist on putting a portion of the purchase consideration in an escrow account for the duration of the indemnification.

In an all-cash deal, you should be prepared for a buyer to insist on an escrow. An escrow account is the buyer's only real assurance that money will be around to satisfy his claims. The amount of the escrow is generally dependent on how comfortable the buyer is with the strength and veracity of your representations and warranties. By no means, however, should you allow an escrow to amount to more that 20 per cent of the purchase consideration (the percentage gets smaller as the deal size increases). All escrow accounts should be interest-bearing and should be administered by a third party.

We typically attempt to arrange for an increasing percentage of the escrow to be released to the seller as time passes and the threat of major misrepresentation lessens. Under no circumstances should the escrow extend beyond the duration of the indemnification.

In a transaction that involves a significant deferred pay out, such as a note or an earn-out, an escrow becomes less vital to a buyer. In the event that significant damages do arise in such circumstances, buyers generally establish their claims against those deferred payments. In essence, those payments act as the escrow.

THE CLOSING

The closing is the actual event in which a transaction is consummated through the execution of all documentation and the transfer of title or stock in exchange for a like transfer of funds.

In most instances, the closing day will be as hectic and chaotic as any you will have ever encountered. Every group that is a party to the deal will be at the closing, along with their respective advisers. There may be dozens of people involved with the actual closing: from you and the buyer, to the buyer's lender and certain of your debt or lien holders. This, of course, can cause a logistical as well as an administrative nightmare. The buyer's legal team will generally be responsible for coordinating all of the documentation and the sequence of events.

You should be certain that all closing documents are negotiated, reviewed and approved well before the day of closing. The closing should be a mere formality. You do not want to let the buyer have any opportunity to renegotiate the deal or wangle out of any obligations.

Well in advance of the closing day, your legal adviser should provide you with the litany of documents you will need to bring to the closing, including the stock certificates, articles of incorporation, corporate minute book and tax records, to name but a few. In addition, you need to give yourself and your advisers adequate time to compile and prepare all necessary exhibits, schedules and other information you will need for the purchase document.

We were recently involved with a seller whose lack of foresight and planning in these matters caused him to lose a deal. The seller owned a clothing company which marketed its products under various brand names. Both he and the buyer thought all the names were trademarked – obviously a very important factor in protecting the brands. The seller's lawyer fell behind in preparing various exhibits to the purchase document. Rather than delay the closing, both sides agreed to review the missing exhibits on the day of the closing. Unfortunately, one of these exhibits was the documentation relating to the trademarks. To our client's surprise and the buyer's dismay, one of the brands was not trademarked – it was free to be used by any manufacturer.

The buyer was more upset by the fact that the seller did not have a grasp on his business than the fact that the brand was not trademarked. Clearly, the buyer must have wondered what other troubling aspects of the business went unnoticed or unknown by the seller.

There is no doubt that if our client had coordinated the compilation of the exhibits in a more organized manner, he would have discovered the problem well before the day of closing and would have had time to deal with it. The element of surprise, more than anything else, killed the deal.

It is important to remember that you are not just executing documents at the closing; you are also transferring your entire business to another party. It is advisable to meet with your legal team a few times before the actual closing so that you are familiar with all of the various documents and your obligations at the closing.

Most acquisitions require cash payments to be made by certified cheque, bank cashier's cheque or wire transfer. If given a choice, we generally have a bias for wire transfers. Cheques, even certified cheques, require time to clear. A certified cheque merely assures the recipient that the payer's account has sufficient funds; no guarantee is made as to when the funds will clear and be transferred to the recipient' s account. A wire transfer, however, is a computerized transfer of funds and provides an immediate credit of the funds to the seller's account.

Most sellers insist on having all cash payments made by wire transfer. In situations where the consideration is large and overnight interest is significant, wire transfers make economic sense. After all, why give the buyer the overnight float on the money? In addition, wire transfers provide the comfort of knowing that the funds are immediately and safely in the bank.

Many owners have told us that they find the pressures and anxiety of the closing process to be extremely stressful. None the less, it is important to keep some perspective on the matter. After all, the closing is the culmination of a long and arduous process; a closing will also bring with it a tremendous amount of exhilaration, relief and, best of all, money.

Case Study: Advanced Technologies Inc

Perhaps the clearest way to summarize all the points we have raised in this book is to present a case study of a company that recently went through the process of selling. This study will succinctly demonstrate how the selling process works, in addition to highlighting the trials and tribulations inherent in any sale of a business. In order to protect our client's privacy, we have changed the names of the companies and individuals involved, as well as modified the description of the company's operations. The story, however, remains representative of the process.

DESCRIPTION OF THE COMPANY AND BRIEF HISTORY

Advanced Technologies Inc manufactures a proprietary line of aluminium castings for the automotive and business machine industries. Located in Toledo, Ohio, the company is a recognized leader in its field and has established a strong reputation for the quality of its products and its innovative approach to engineering problems.

Advanced was founded in 1970 by James Smith, when he was 55 years old. Soon afterward, his only son, Chris, joined the company. By 1985, Chris had assumed the role of President, as his father began to spend more of his time in Florida. By 1990, the company had grown to over $5 million of annual sales, and James Smith had gifted all of his stock in equal proportions to his son, Chris, and his three daughters.

In 1995, Chris Smith saw a need for a stronger management team to guide the company into the future. After an exhaustive search, he hired an Executive Vice-president, Tom Ward, who had extensive experience running a large division of a Fortune 500 company in a similar industry. Tom Ward was attracted to Advanced because of its superior reputation and its growth potential. Another, even greater, attraction was that Chris Smith was 62 and nearing retirement age. At

45, Tom Ward was hired with the explicit understanding that he would become the CEO within three years.

Tom Ward had an immediate impact on the company. He expanded the product offerings into new fields and introduced more efficient production techniques to the plant. Tom also knew how to delegate responsibility, and he soon began to recruit a strong second-tier of management to back him up. Most importantly, Tom was able to introduce change without disrupting the company's steady growth or profitability.

In 1997, Chris Smith retired, and Tom Ward assumed the company's Presidency. The company continued to grow and prosper under Tom's tutelage. A summary of its financial performance is provided below:

Table 9.1

Operating results – Advanced Technologies Inc

($000s)

PROJ.

	FYE 12/31/99	FYE 12/31/98	FYE 12/31/97	FYE 12/31/96	FYE 12/31/95
Net Sales	$35,000	$30,600	$27,400	$24,700	$20,100
CAGR	14.4%	11.7%	10.9%	22.8%	—
Gross Profit	$11,200	$9,730	$8,900	$7,780	$6,210
Gross Margin	32.0%	31.8%	32.5%	31.5%	30.9%
Profit Before Tax and Discretionary Costs*	$4,200	$3,670	$3,425	$2,840	$2,210
Profit Before Tax	$3,600	$3,070	$2,825	$2,240	$1,610

CAGR = Compound Annual Growth Rate
* Includes salaries and directors' fees paid to members of the Smith family

The company also had a strong balance sheet, as the Smith family had a policy of reinvesting most of the company's earnings back into the company. The balance sheet is summarized below, as of the fiscal year ending 31 December 1998:

Table 9.2

Balance sheet – Advanced Technologies Inc

	$(000s) As of 12/31/98
ASSETS	
Current Assets	$9,395
Current Liabilities	$4,685
Net Working Capital	$4,710
Property and Equipment:	
Cost	$9,870
Accumulated Depreciation	$3,730
Net Fixed Assets	$6,140
Other Assets	$250
Total Assets	$11,100
LIABILITIES AND EQUITY	
Long-term Debt	$2,650
Stockholders' Equity	$8,450
Total Capitalization	$11,100

DAY 1: 5 JANUARY 1999

In keeping with tradition, the Smith family held its annual Board meeting just after the holidays. As CEO, Tom Ward presided over the meeting. He reviewed the company's performance in 1998 and its prospects for the new year. Tom foresaw a great future for the company. Indeed, just a few months earlier, two potential customers had approached Tom about significant new business opportunities, both of which would commence by 2Q 1999. Yet, to capitalize on these opportunities and to generally stay competitive, Tom was convinced that it was going to be necessary to spend $3.5 million over the next two years to expand the plant. The company had a strong balance sheet and could afford to borrow the money.

Janet Klein, Chris Smith's eldest sister, looked visibly startled. Each sibling had been receiving $150,000 a year as a Director's fee. She explained that she had planned to petition the Board for an increased payment. Now that her husband was retired, she counted on this income to support them. Her youngest daughter had decided to return to college, and Mrs Klein had plans to buy a small weekend house. Suddenly, her income from the company was not enough.

Several of the other siblings also expressed an interest in increasing their income from the company. Tom Ward explained that cash flow would be very tight if the expansion plans were carried out and that the family's income would more probably have to be decreased, not increased.

After the question of expansion versus income was briefly debated, Chris Smith put forward the idea of selling the company. Just a few months earlier, he had received an unsolicited approach from a Chicago-based investment group called Charles Holdings. Chris explained that as no family member was still involved in the company, a move like this would probably not upset their 83-year-old father too much.

Perhaps selling was the answer to their dilemma: it would allow the shareholders their liquidity, without burdening the company's expansion plans. After some discussion, the rest of the family appeared quite interested in exploring this matter. Tom Ward was given the mandate to investigate and report back to the family.

DAY 10: 15 JANUARY 1999

Tom Ward had spent the last few days compiling information on investment banks to help the family explore this issue further. He had narrowed his list down to three candidates: the capital markets division of his local bank, a regional investment bank and our firm. On 15 January Tom called our office. He said we had been recommended by a former client and invited us to visit him and look at his operation.

After reviewing the company's financial statements and marketing materials, we made plans to travel to Toledo to spend the day with Tom and to see the company.

DAY 14: 19 JANUARY 1999

Tom Ward picked us up at the airport around 10:00 am. We drove to the main plant, where we were to spend the day. As we came in the office, Tom casually announced to the receptionist that we were a New York-based consulting firm that he had hired to do some market research for the company. This remained our 'cover identity' for the entire time we worked for the company.

We spent the next hour walking through the plant and were very pleased with what we saw. The facilities were clean, and the employees appeared to be hard working. There were many efficiency awards posted, as well as letters of excellence from customers. The next few hours were spent reviewing the company's history, current perform-ance and future prospects. We also discussed all the elements we would need to prepare the descriptive memorandum, should the company decide to retain us.

During a late lunch, we met Chris Smith and Janet Klein, Chris Smith's sister. After some brief conversation, we got down to the crux of the matter: they were interested in what we thought the business was worth.

Fortunately, prior to the meeting, Tom had provided us with five years of historical statements, as well as three years of projections. We reviewed with Chris Smith and his sister the current state of the market, and the specific prospects for the company going forward. We concluded that we believed that a 6–6.5 multiple of projected, re-constructed FY 1999 pre-tax profits could be achieved, assuming we were able to create an active market for the company. This equated to a value of $25–27 million.

After lunch we had a brief tour of the company's adjacent facility, and then Tom took us back to the airport. He said he would be in touch with us.

DAY 24: 29 JANUARY 1999

Tom had called us several days earlier to say that his personal choice was for us to represent the company, but that the ultimate decision rested with the Board. He wanted us to meet the Board in Toledo to make a presentation. We accepted the invitation and, on the afternoon of 30 January we met with the entire Board: Chris Smith and his three sisters.

After introducing ourselves, we gave a brief history of our firm and discussed our operating philosophy and approach to the market. We handed out references of several owners whose firms we had recently sold. Next, we discussed the company's prospects. We presented our valuation range and explained how we had arrived at it.

We turned then to the most important part of the meeting: a general discussion of how all the shareholders felt about selling the company. Although we had ostensibly been invited to the Board meeting after a decision to sell had already been made, we knew from prior experience that, more likely than not, there was no unanimity of opinion. As it turned out, the situation with Advanced Technologies was no exception.

Anne James, the youngest sibling, was very much against selling altogether. She was a very successful real estate broker, married to an entrepreneur, who clearly did not need the income she received from the company. She felt that the company was part of the family, and that selling it would be like selling a part of themselves. Besides, as a major employer in town, the company provided the entire family with a certain amount of prestige.

Janet Klein had had several weeks to think about selling the company since the matter had come up at the annual Board meeting. She owned 25 per cent of the stock. If the company was worth as much as $25 million, she would receive $6 million pre-tax. Investing that amount in municipal bonds would yield over $250,000 in tax-free annual income - significantly more than what she was getting now. Furthermore, the return was guaranteed and not predicated on the good fortune of the company. Alternatively, her capital would be made liquid, free to be spent if she so chose. She and her husband were very interested in selling.

Beth Kellogg, the middle daughter, and her husband were both teachers. While they enjoyed having the income from the company, they lived a rather modest life, and in fact saved most of their discretionary income. Beth was indifferent regarding the sale. She believed that it would be easier from an estate perspective if her holdings in the company were liquid. However, since she was only 55 and in good health, she was not overly concerned about this matter. The one point that did matter to her was that she did not want the sale of the company to divide the family. She could already see the battle lines being drawn between Anne and Janet.

Like his sister Janet, Chris Smith realized that his income would increase dramatically by selling the company. But, like his sister Anne, he knew it would be difficult for him to participate in the sale of the business his father started.

However, Chris had another, larger problem on his mind. His wife, Caroline, had heard a rumour from some mutual friends that Tom Ward had recently been offered the presidency of a much larger company. Chris was quite aware that Tom had become essential to the company's future and, therefore, the value of the business. It was Tom who engineered the tremendous growth in revenues and profitability over the previous five years. Chris was not at all certain that he could return to run the company should Tom leave. Even if he could, he had absolutely no desire to return from his comfortable retirement to do so. Chris Smith realized that he *had* to pursue a sale, if only to continue to provide Tom Ward with a stimulating and challenging work environment.

For an hour, each of the siblings presented their points of view. The discussion went round and round with no resolution being reached. Finally, Anne suggested they call their father who, after all, had started the company. Although James Smith was now in his 80s, his mind was still very quick. We left the room while the siblings called their father in Florida. Much to everyone's surprise, James Smith was quite determined that the company be sold. He saw a sale as the one way to adequately secure the future for all his children and grand-children. That, more than just the company, would be his legacy.

Just as important to James Smith, however, were the advantages of a sale to both Advanced Technologies and Tom Ward. James Smith felt strongly that no company could stand still and remain competitive. The family either had to commit to fund the continued expansion of Advanced, or decide to sell. It was unfair to both James Smith, who had founded the company, and Tom Ward, who had truly built the company, to hold it back.

We were summoned back to the meeting and given the mandate to sell the company. Our agreement stated that we would represent Advanced Technologies on an exclusive basis for six months. We left Tom Ward with a list of items we would need in order to prepare the descriptive memorandum.

DAY 41: 15 FEBRUARY 1999

Tom Ward had sent the information we had requested within the week and by 15 February we had a working first draft of the prospectus.

We had also prepared an initial list of 60 potential acquirers whom we wanted to approach. This list was narrowed down from a larger universe of 350 parties we deemed as likely candidates. These potential buyers included European and Asian firms, large domestic companies in related fields and a few well-capitalized private investment groups. The list did not include any companies in the broad castings field or any direct competitors. Our goal was to keep the process confidential and handle the approaches with discretion. A separate list of com-petitors was drawn up. The family and we could decide at a later date whether to approach these parties.

DAY 48: 22 FEBRUARY 1999

We were now on the third and final draft of the selling memorandum. The list had been reviewed, and three parties had been excluded, because Tom Ward had had personal dealings with each of these firms and was not comfortable with their management styles.

We began to make discreet direct approaches to the potential buyers on the list. We contacted the appropriate person at each company and discussed their acquisition goals. If the conversation sounded promising, we described our client in general terms, without providing any specifics. We only released detailed information after a confidentiality agreement had been executed.

Of the 57 companies we approached, 25 were interested in receiving more information. After they executed confidentiality agreements, we provided them with the descriptive memorandum.

While we were pleased with our initial response rate (44 per cent), our goal was to send out at least 40 reports. From our first set of calls, it appeared that the parties most interested in Advanced Technologies were those in related fields, so we returned to our initial universe of potential suitors and chose an additional 40 parties to approach.

From this second group of candidates, an additional 20 companies (50 per cent) requested the selling memorandum.

DAY 66: 12 MARCH 1999

Of the 45 companies that received the report, five had already returned it. One was not interested because they did not like the company's concentration of customers in the automotive field. Another discovered from the report that the company had a union, a definite negative to them.

By this point, we had been in touch with all of the suitors that had received the report. Several had requested some additional information, many had only reviewed the report once and were not ready to comment, and a few were interested in visiting Tom Ward and examining the facilities.

We arranged the first meeting for 12 March; Tom Ward met us and David Wilding, the Chairman of International Stamping plc at the airport. International Stamping was a $400 million manufacturer of various metal components, with headquarters in London. In 1998, International Stamping had made an acquisition of a Detroit-based firm with a complementary product line. They had been pleased with their first American acquisition and were eager to continue expanding in the US.

Tom took us back to the plant and again told the receptionist that we were all involved in new market research. Mr Wilding was taken on a tour of the plant. He seemed visibly impressed with what he saw and complimented Tom on his operation. David Wilding had prepared a list of questions he wanted to review, which he had forwarded to us before the meeting. Tom had compiled a very impressive presentation which addressed all of Wilding's questions. In general, Tom was very responsive, direct and cooperative, as well as being enthusiastic.

After the meeting, we were convinced that the day had gone well. Tom was a positive seller, who was able to present the company in its best possible light. At the airport, Mr Wilding confirmed our perceptions; he said that he would definitely get back to us with an offer. He inquired whether other companies were interested in buying Advanced, as he had a policy against getting involved in bidding wars. We assured him that he was the first to visit, and that no one else had made an offer.

DAY 80: 26 MARCH 1999

True to his word, David Wilding called us a couple of weeks after his visit and made a verbal offer of $20 million. We were disappointed. Not only did we believe the total offer to be low, but only $17 million of the bid was for cash. Of the remaining $3 million, $2 million was to be paid as a non-compete payment over five years, with the final $1 million to be paid at the end of two years if Advanced's profits grew at a 15 per cent rate over that period. Using a 10 per cent discount rate, we valued the $3 million future payments to be worth only a little more than $2 million. Hence, if the shareholders were to receive all of the future payments, the total equated to a present value of $19 million.

We responded to Wilding that we thought the offer was low. However, we did suggest that he put the offer in writing, and we would take it to the family. Wilding was quite accommodating, but instructed us that he was not interested in having his deal shopped around. He wanted a quick response.

We recognized that this was going to be a problem. The prior week, Bud Clark had visited the company and was excited about expanding into Advanced's product lines. Clark was the President of Lindsay Industries, a NYSE-listed, Pittsburgh-based manufacturer of plastic and metal components, with revenues of $775 million. Furthermore, we had three other companies scheduled to visit over the next three weeks. While we certainly were not going to play by Wilding's rules, we did have to be careful in how we handled the matter going forward. After a conference with Tom Ward, we decided to suspend the search for more parties and concentrate instead on creating a market from those parties currently examining Advanced. If the market fizzled out, we could always go back to the well.

DAY 101: 16 APRIL 1999

Three weeks had passed since David Wilding had made his initial offer. Shortly after he presented his letter of intent, we responded that the family felt the total offer was too low and that the deal structure left too much of the purchase price on the back-end. Wilding countered that he would increase the cash by $1 million. After a few days wait, we once again told him that the offer was too low. He responded by increasing the cash by an additional $1 million, but added that the offer was his final one and would be outstanding only until 20 April. He sensed we were stalling for time, and he was right.

Meanwhile, after some discreet negotiating, Lindsay Industries had also made an offer. They proposed a stock-for-stock swap, valuing Advanced at $26 million. Lindsay's stock had shown steady but consistent growth, and paid a 3 per cent dividend. An attractive feature of this offer was that, as a stock deal, the shareholders could defer any tax liability until they sold their Lindsay stock. If they sold only a portion of the Lindsay stock, they would be taxed only on that portion.

Three other parties had also visited over the last two weeks. A well-capitalized investor group, with a similar casting operation in California, had visited two weeks earlier. They seemed impressed at the meeting, but later called to say that Advanced was not a good fit with their operation. We were quite surprised, as Tom Ward believed that the two businesses truly complemented each other.

Herbert Orvis of Charles Holdings, the investment group that originally approached Chris Smith and acted as a catalyst to the entire matter, called Chris again. Chris put them in touch with us, and they too had spent a day with Tom examining the business.

Finally, Canam, a large, private diversified Canadian company visited. The President of Canam's castings division, Ken Francis, was very complimentary about the company in general and Tom Ward in particular. Canam wanted to expand into the US. They had already looked at several American companies, but none had been up to their standards. Ken Francis felt that they could bring a lot to Advanced, and that Advanced would offer them an ideal entree into the American market. However, the decision was not Francis' to make; the chairman of Canam had the final say, as he owned and had an active interest in it. The Chairman could not visit the company for at least two weeks.

DAY 121: 6 MAY 1999

Canam's chairman had spent the day with Tom Ward about two weeks after Ken Francis' visit. Tom had been very impressed with him and had agreed to visit Canam's castings operation in Canada. Ken Francis remained upbeat, but still had not made an offer. When pressured, he would put us off. 'Take another offer if you must,' he would say. 'This is a big decision for us, and we must be certain it is the right one.' We decided to retreat from pressing too hard for fear he would walk.

Meanwhile we had gone back to David Wilding at International Stamping plc and told him we had an offer for $26 million. We did not mention that the offer was from Lindsay or that it was in stock. Naturally, Wilding was upset. However, he did not drop his offer, as he had threatened to do, but rather he increased it to $25 million in cash, with a $3 million non-compete payment paid at the end of five years. Using a 10 per cent discount rate, this offer was worth approximately $27 million.

Charles Holdings remained interested in Advanced, but they had a problem coming up with the cash. Because they were going to borrow a substantial portion of the purchase price, they could only arrange a cash payment of $18 million. Having been told of the offer for $26 million, Herbert Orvis of Charles claimed that they could top our best offer by $1.0 million. They offered the following: $18 million in cash; $5 million in seven-year notes paying 10 per cent interest; and a $3.0 million contingent payment to be paid at the end of three years if the company met certain earnings tests. In addition, they offered to let the family keep a 10 per cent ownership in the company.

Tom Ward was resolutely against selling to Charles. He recognized that the investment group might make the family the highest offer. However, by leveraging the balance sheet, they would also impair Ward's ability to expand his operations. The next five years would be spent concentrating on paying the debt, not growing the company. Despite his reservations about Charles, Tom accepted the fact that the decision was ultimately the family's, and he kept his opinions to himself.

DAY 128: 13 MAY 1999

We had reached the day of reckoning. We had two good offers from groups that both Tom Ward and the family felt would take the company forward and help continue its growth. Both International Stamping and Lindsay were pressing us for an answer. We also had the offer from Charles Holdings, which was for a higher nominal value and had an added benefit of allowing the family to keep an interest in the company.

However, Tom felt that Canam was such a strong potential partner that he did not want the family to make a decision without hearing from them. At Tom's urging, we called Ken Francis at Canam. We mentioned that we did not want to force his hand, but that the family had several other offers and were being pressed to take one. Francis asked us what our best offer was. We told him that there was a bid of $27 million, not mentioning the structure. He responded that he would call us back.

That afternoon, Ken Francis called. He stated that Canam was pleased to offer $30 million in cash for Advanced. He further said he was not interested in negotiating, that his bid was more than fair, especially given the considerable additional investment that would be required to grow Advanced. In fact, Francis said that Canam was only willing to pay such a high price because the company was very well run and offered Canam a unique opportunity to get into the US market.

After telling the family of the Canam offer, we immediately called David Wilding at International Stamping, as well as Herb Orvis at Charles Holdings and Bud Clark at Lindsay. Herb Orvis and David Wilding could do no better. However, Bud Clark said he was prepared to revise his offer subject to board approval. He said that he would be back to us by the end of the day. At around 6:00 pm, Clark called. He could offer $30 million in stock, but he demanded a final decision within two days.

DAY 132: 17 MAY 1999

A special Board meeting of Advanced Technologies had been called to discuss the offers. Each had its merits and deserved careful consideration. As the family members sat down at the table, we gave them a sheet which summarized the offers:

Table 9.3

Summary of offers for Advanced Technologies Inc – 17 May 1999

BIDDER	UPFRONT CASH/STOCK	MAXIMUM SUBSEQUENT PAYMENTS	MAXIMUM TOTAL PRESENT VALUE
INTL. STAMPING	$25 million cash	$3 million	$27 million
LINDSAY IND.	$30 million stock		$30 million
CHARLES HLDGS.	$18 million cash	$8 million	$25 million (1)
CANAM	$30 million cash		$30 million

(1) Shareholders also retain 10 per cent of company

All agreed that the International Stamping and Charles Holdings offers were not as good as the others, either in total value or structure. Anne James was tempted by Charles' offer because she liked the idea of keeping part of the company. But she realized the heavy debt burden would make it difficult to continue to grow the company. Everyone also rejected the 'back-end' contingent nature of the Charles offer.

Both the Lindsay and Canam offers were for the same amount; both were secured offers. The only real difference was the form of payment. Lindsay's stock deal would allow the shareholders to defer taxes, perhaps indefinitely. Yet, it did concentrate all of their wealth in one stock, providing no real diversity. Also, the dividend was only 3 per cent. After much discussion, all four family members declared themselves neutral. They asked Tom Ward for his thoughts.

Tom stated that either suitor would be acceptable to him. Both wanted to grow the company, and both were committed to supplying him with the resources to do so. However, he personally believed Canam's management style to be more in accord with his own. He felt much more comfortable with their managers and their approach to business. If it was his decision, he would choose Canam.

The family members voted one by one... all in favour of Canam. We were instructed to call Ken Francis and accept the bid. As we left to do so, Anne James started to cry.

DAY 155: 9 JUNE 1999

We had been very pleased with how the selling process had worked thus far. The market generated several fine offers. Tom Ward was happy with the pending acquirer, and the offer was at the high end of our expected range. However, we had premonitions that the closing process was not to be a smooth one when, two weeks after agreeing to the deal, the family still had not executed the letter of intent.

What had started out as a minor issue in the letter of intent had escalated into a huge impasse. Canam had included a standard clause that the shareholders would indemnify Canam against any unknown and undisclosed liabilities that had occurred while they had owned the company. As we have discussed in Chapter 8, this is a customary request by a buyer. No acquirer wants to be liable for unknown or undisclosed problems that surface after the sale.

For 20 years, both Chris Smith and the company had used a small, local law firm for all of their legal work. The firm specialized in estate planning and real estate law. When Bill Lam, the partner in charge, reviewed the letter of intent, he protested strongly against the indemnity clause. He argued that the shareholders should under no circumstances agree to indemnify off-balance sheet liabilities.

In an attempt to circumvent this impasse, Canam decided to start writing the purchase agreement, without executing a letter of intent. They hoped that the Advanced shareholders (and their lawyer) would be more reasonable if they got further into the negotiating process. However, Ken Francis was very irritated. He wondered if the lawyer had a hidden agenda and did not really want the family to sell. It was clearly evident that Advanced was an important client to Bill Lam's firm. Francis wondered whether Lam was creating an untenable road-block merely to scuttle the deal and retain an important client.

DAY 245: 7 SEPTEMBER 1999

Matters went from bad to worse. Not only was Bill Lam finding more and more things wrong with what appeared to be a reasonable purchase agreement, but the company's performance was slipping. One of Advanced's large customers had not come through with a big order that Tom had anticipated. Tom had revised his projected FY 1999 reconstructed pre-tax profits from $4.2 million to $3.8 million.

Meanwhile, the indemnity issue was still not resolved. Ken Francis had agreed to limit the amount of potential liability to $10 million (at one-third the purchase price, a very unusual concession), and agreed to there being no escrow. Mr Lam was still arguing for no indemnification whatsoever.

Both the family and we were more concerned about the earnings drop than the arguments over the purchase agreement. We fully expected Ken Francis to move to lower the price, given the drastic decrease in earnings and the fact that the deal reflected a healthy multiple of projected earnings already. To our surprise and relief, Ken did not try to renegotiate the deal. This, more than anything, evidenced Canam's deep desire to buy Advanced.

However, Ken Francis did use the deterioration in earnings to his advantage. He came back to the family and claimed that he would not negotiate the deal any further until the family retained another law firm to help Mr Lam complete the deal.

While he did not want to remove their long trusted counsel, Ken Francis insisted that the family also use a larger firm with specific experience in mergers and acquisitions. At this point, the family was getting irritated with Bill Lam. Chris Smith, who was spearheading the operation, saw no serious risk in the indemnification. After all, it only covered liabilities which were undisclosed. The company had audited statements and did not have any outstanding litigation or environmental problems. They were always open and forthright about how they ran their business, and had been equally so in the due diligence with Canam. In the end, he was actually relieved to be able to hire outside counsel, and immediately did so.

DAY 265: 27 SEPTEMBER 1999

In less than two weeks, all of the issues relating to the purchase agreement were resolved. The family accepted the $10 million indemnification exposure and almost nine months after the family had started to think about selling, the deal was done.

At the close, Chris Smith was nostalgic. Afterward, he made a brief speech to the employees and thanked them for their loyal service. Then he turned the programme over to Ken Francis. Ken told everyone how excited he was about the company's prospects, and how pleased he was that Advanced was now part of the Canam family.

POSTSCRIPT

We called Tom Ward six months after the closing to see how business was fairing. He sounded very upbeat. Canam had steered over $5.0 million of new businesses to him. They had also committed to fund a $4.0 million plant expansion in the new year. Because he was being paid a substantial bonus based on performance, Tom was quite excited about both his and Advanced's continuing prospects.

We also talked to Chris Smith a year later. While he felt a bit sad that his family no longer owned the company, he had moved to Florida, was enjoying his new motor boat, and was about to fly to Australia for a six-week vacation. On reflection, Chris exclaimed that the sale worked out quite well indeed for both him and his sisters.

APPENDIX I

Sample Confidentiality Agreements

CONFIDENTIALITY AGREEMENT 1

PERSONAL AND CONFIDENTIAL   1 March 1999

Mr William Smith
President
Potential Buyer plc
100 Industrial Road
Any City AB12 3CD

Dear Mr Smith,

This is to confirm the interest of Potential Buyer plc in examining the business of Potential Seller plc or certain of its operations ('the company'). In connection with such examination, you will be furnished with certain financial statements and other information and documents relating to the company and its business. In consideration of the conduct of such examination, Potential Buyer plc will keep in strict confidence and will not, directly or indirectly, divulge (i) the fact that such an examination is being conducted or (ii) any of the financial and other information furnished to us by you.

Potential Buyer plc acknowledges that documents furnished to you by us contain confidential information which will at all times remain the exclusive property of the company. You further acknowledge that you will be responsible for the safekeeping of these documents and will not reproduce, disseminate or otherwise disclose the information contained therein to any third parties.

You acknowledge that the company would sustain irreparable injury in the event of a breach of this agreement by Potential Buyer plc. Accordingly, in the event of any such breach, the company will be entitled to seek and obtain immediate injunctive relief against Potential

Buyer plc. This agreement will be binding on Potential Buyer plc, its employees, directors and representatives.

Respectfully,

Potential Seller plc

_____

Mr Alan Jones
President

Confirmed and agreed:

Potential Buyer plc

_____

Mr William Smith
President

Date: _____

CONFIDENTIALITY AGREEMENT 2

PERSONAL AND CONFIDENTIAL   1 March 1999

Mr William Smith
President
Potential Buyer plc
100 Industrial Road
Any City AB12 3CD

Dear Mr Smith,

In connection with your consideration of a possible acquisition of Potential Seller plc ('the company'), you (including all affiliated entities) have requested information concerning the company. As a condition to your being furnished such information, you hereby agree to treat any information concerning the company (whether oral or written and whether prepared by or on behalf of the company) which is furnished to you by or on behalf of the company (herein collectively referred to as the 'Evaluation Material') in accordance with the provisions of this letter, and to take or refrain from taking certain other actions herein set forth. The term 'Evaluation Material' does not include information which (i) is already in your possession, provided that such information is not known by you to be subject to another confidentiality agreement with the company, or (ii) becomes generally available to the public other than as a result of a disclosure by you or your directors, officers, employees, or advisors (collectively 'Representatives'), or (iii) becomes available to you on a non-confidential basis from a source other than the company or its Representatives, provided that such source is not known by you to be bound by a confidentiality agreement with the company or another party.

You hereby agree that the Evaluation Material will be used solely for the purpose of evaluating a possible transaction between the company and you, and that such information will be kept confidential by you and your Representatives; provided, however, that any of such information may be disclosed to your Representatives who need to know such information for the purpose of evaluating any such possible transaction (it being understood that such directors, officers, employees and advisers shall be informed by you of the confidential nature of such information and shall be directed by you to treat such information confidentially). You further agree to be responsible for any breach of this agreement by your Representatives.

In addition, without the prior written consent of the company, you will not, and will direct such Representatives not to, disclose to any person either the fact that discussions or negotiations are taking place concerning a possible transaction between the company and you or any of the terms, conditions or other facts with respect to any such possible transaction, including the status thereof.

Although the company has endeavoured to include in the Evaluation Material information known to it which it believes to be relevant for the purpose of your investigation, you understand that neither the company nor their advisers have made or make any representation or warranty as to the accuracy or completeness of the Evaluation Material. You agree that neither the company nor their advisers shall have any liability to you resulting from the use of the Evaluation Material.

In the event that you do not proceed with the transaction which is the subject of this letter within a reasonable time frame, you shall promptly redeliver to the company (and in any event shall promptly redeliver to the company upon request) all written Evaluation Material and any other written material containing any information in or derived from the Evaluation Material, and will not retain any copies, extracts or other reproductions in whole or in part of such written material.

As a condition to providing you with the Evaluation Material, you hereby agree that until one year from the date hereof, you and your Representatives will not solicit to hire any person employed by the company.

It is understood that the company may institute appropriate proceedings against you to enforce its rights hereunder. You hereby confirm that the company shall be entitled to specific performance and injunctive relief as remedies for any violation of this Agreement. These remedies shall not be deemed to be the exclusive remedies for a violation of the terms of this Agreement, but shall be in addition to all other remedies available to the company at law or equity.

This letter shall be governed by, and construed and enforced in accordance with, the laws of the England.

If you are in agreement with the foregoing, please sign and return one copy of the letter.

Very truly yours,

Potential Seller plc

By: _____
Mr Alan Jones
President

Confirmed and agreed:

Potential Buyer plc

By: _____
Mr William Smith
President

Date: _____

A P P E N D I X   I I

Sample Letters of Intent

LETTER OF INTENT 1

PERSONAL AND CONFIDENTIAL   1 March 1999

Mr Alan Jones
President
Potential Seller plc
36 Main Street
Any City XX11 4ZZ

Dear Mr Jones:

We are pleased to submit this letter to you as an outline by which Potential Buyer plc ('Buyer'), or its assigns, proposes to purchase the common stock of Potential Seller plc ('Seller'). The key terms of our proposal are as follows:

Cash Payment:	£22 million cash at closing.
Seller Note:	£3 million in a 10 per cent Seller Note. Interest will be payable quarterly. Principal shall be payable thirty-six months from closing.
Bank Debt:	Seller shall have no bank debt as of the closing. To the extent that Seller has any interest-bearing debt at closing, the amount of such debt shall be netted from the cash payment.
Minimum Net Worth:	At closing, the net worth of Seller must be at least £8.5 million.
Employment Arrangements:	Mutually satisfactory employment arrangements detailing salary and bonus

opportunities will be negotiated with current management. It is our desire and intention that Seller's key employees continue with the business. Mr Alan Jones will be retained as an employee for a minimum of one year at a salary base of £200 000 annually, with a bonus of up to £50 000 based on certain operating performance measures being met.

Exclusivity: Seller and its financial advisors agree to discontinue all efforts to sell the company to other potential purchasers during a 90 day period beginning the date this letter of intent is accepted.

Closing: On or before 30 May 1999.

Escrow: £1 million for period of one year from closing, against all claims arising in excess of £250 000.

Insurance: Mr Alan Jones to have the right to purchase any insurance owned by the Company at its book value.

In submitting this letter of intent to you, it is our intention that it is not to be legally binding (except for the Exclusivity clause), but is subject to due diligence and the negotiation, execution and delivery of a definitive purchase agreement satisfactory in form and substance to each of us and our respective counsel.

Should this proposal be acceptable, please sign the enclosed copy and return it to us at your earliest convenience.

Best regards.

Sincerely,

Potential Buyer plc

_____

Mr William Smith

Agreed and accepted:

Potential Seller plc

_____

Mr Alan Jones

Date: _____

LETTER OF INTENT 2

Mr Alan Jones   1 March 1999
President
Potential Seller plc
36 Main Street
Any City XX11 4ZZ

Dear Mr. Jones,

Re: Offer to purchase outstanding capital stock of Potential Seller plc

This letter sets forth the basis upon which Potential Buyer plc ('Buyer') proposes to purchase all of the outstanding capital stock of Potential Seller plc ('Seller').

1. The acquisition will be effected by the purchase of all of the outstanding capital stock of Seller (the 'Stock'). Buyer will pay an aggregate purchase price of $25.0 million as adjusted as hereinafter provided (the 'Purchase Price') for the Stock to the stockholders of Seller, pro rata (the 'Selling Stockholders') in the following manner:

   (a) An aggregate of $22.0 million will be paid by certified check or wire transfer of funds at closing.
   (b) An aggregate of $3.0 million will be paid by promissory note, which shall provide for the payment of 12 equal quarterly instalments of $250 000 plus accrued interest on the unpaid balance each quarter at an interest rate of 10 per cent.
   (c) An aggregate of $1.0 million (the 'Escrow Fund') will be deposited in escrow by Seller at closing with a mutually acceptable financial institution to provide a fund for (i) the adjustment

to the Purchase Price occasioned by the post closing audit set forth below, or (ii) any claims for indemnity arising out of breaches of the representations and warranties of the Selling Stockholders over $250 000 as set forth in the definitive agreement. The balance of the Escrow Fund, with interest, after appropriate adjustments and claims have been paid to Buyer, will be distributed to the Selling Stockholders, pro rata, one year from the date of closing. In addition, Buyer will immediately pay into the Escrow Fund such additional principal sums as may be required to reflect an adjustment in the Purchase Price to a sum greater than $22.0 million as a result of such post closing audit.

2. This offer is subject to the following conditions precedent:

(a) There shall have been no material change in the business or material adverse change in Seller's financial condition since 31 December 1998 to the date of closing. Assuming that the closing of the transaction occurs on or as of 30 May 1999, a 30 May 1999 balance sheet will be prepared as soon as practicable following the closing in accordance with generally accepted accounting principles applied in a manner consistent with the principles used by Seller for purposes of preparing its 31 December 1998 audited balance sheet. Such balance sheet shall be subject to review by the Selling Stockholders and shall contain the opinion of Seller's accountants. The definitive agreement referred to in subparagraph (b) below shall include provisions for the resolution of any disputes regarding such balance sheet. If such 30 May 1999 balance sheet indicates that the net stockholders' equity as of that date was less than $8.5 million, then the Purchase Price will be adjusted downward pound-for-pound by the amount of the deficiency, and if such 30 May 1999 balance sheet indicates that such net stockholders' equity as of that date is greater than $8.5 million, then the Purchase Price will be adjusted upward pound-for-pound by the amount of the excess. The Purchase Price adjustment process described in the preceding sentences will not supersede the representations and warranties or indemnities of the Selling Stockholders set forth in the definitive agreement. If a downward adjustment exceeds the Escrow Fund, Buyer, at its election, may seek indemnity from the Selling Stockholders as permitted by the terms of the definitive agreement outlined below. (b) The execution of a definitive agreement by all Selling Stockholders, which definitive agreement will include, among other things, customary representations, warranties, covenants and indemnities from each party to the others, and opinions of counsel. The customary representations, warranties and covenants will include, without limitations, warranties and covenants of Selling Stockholders as to ownership and transferability of the Stock, the assets, business, financial condition and financial statements of Seller, adequacy of tax payments, the absence of undisclosed liabilities, verifications of machinery and equipment, collectibility of receivables, sufficiency of bad debt reserves, status of litigation, covenants as to continuing conduct of the business and absence of extraordinary payments or material changes since 31 December 1998. The definitive agreement shall also contain provisions addressing the survival of such representations and warranties. Any claims by Buyer for damages arising out of a breach of the representations and warranties shall be several obligations of the Selling Stockholders in proportion to the number of shares owned by each such Selling Stockholder, but will be subject to the customary and mutually acceptable limitations and deductibles.

3. Pending closing, Seller will conduct its business in an ordinary and customary manner.

4. The parties hereto agree that they will use their best efforts to negotiate and execute a definitive agreement relating to the transaction and to prepare all necessary documentation, to obtain all necessary approvals including all stockholder agreements, waivers, consents and clearance, and to complete all other matters relating to this transaction, so as to enable the closing to occur as close to 30 May 1999 as practicable.

5. Pending execution of a definitive agreement, Buyer may perform a due diligence review, during which Buyer's employees and representatives, including legal counsel, accountants, lenders and appraisers, shall have access, at mutually agreed upon times during normal business hours, to the various facilities and operations, to all books and records, and to the employees of Seller, provided that such review is conducted in a manner which will not unreasonably interfere with the conduct of the business of Seller and is consistent with Seller's reasonable requirements to protect confidentiality.

6. Upon execution of this letter and pending the consummation of, and, except for the transactions contemplated hereby, Seller or any of its stockholders will not, and will not permit any of its representatives

to, solicit, encourage or discuss (including by way of furnishing any information concerning its business, properties or assets) any proposal for the acquisition of all or any significant part of Seller's business, properties or assets or any of Seller's capital stock.

7. The parties shall pay their own expenses, including legal advisers', accountants', brokers' or finders' fees and commissions, whether or not the transactions contemplated by this letter are consummated.

8. Neither the Seller, the Buyer nor any of their respective directors, officers, employees or agents shall disclose directly or indirectly the existence or contents of this letter or the negotiation or execution of the Purchase Agreement to any person other than their professional advisors who have a need to know. Additionally, prior to signing the Purchase Agreement, unless required by law or regulation, no public announcement relating to this transaction will be made by the Seller, the Buyer, Shareholder or any affiliated parties. Buyer and Seller each acknowledges that all continuing discussions and negotiations leading to a transaction are still subject to the Confidentiality Agreement dated 7 January 1999 and executed by both parties.

9. This letter, the Purchase Agreement and other definitive agreements will be governed by US law.

10. It is understood that the terms set forth in this letter do not constitute all of the major terms which will be included in the definitive agreement, and that this letter is an expression of intent only and is not intended to create or result in any legally binding obligation upon the parties hereto, except as regards the matters set forth in paragraphs 4, 5, 6, 7, 8, and 9 which shall be binding.

* * * * * * * * *

This offer will expire at 5:00 pm GMT on 10 March 1999 if as of such time, Mr Alan Jones has not executed and delivered a copy of this letter. We, together with our legal and other advisers, are prepared to meet with you and your advisers to resolve any questions you may have.

If you are in agreement with the foregoing, please confirm such agreement by signing and returning to us the enclosed copy of this letter within the specified time period.

Very truly yours,

Potential Buyer plc

By: _____
Mr William Smith
President

Accepted and agreed:

Potential Seller plc

By: _____
Mr Alan Jones
President

Date: _____

Sample Due Diligence Checklist

1. **Organizational structure/history of the company**
   Ownership structure
   Corporate structure (i. e. subsidiaries, divisions)
   Management structure
   Corporate history
2. **Products/Services**
   a. *Types of products*
      Description of product offerings/product lines
      Sales history and market share for each product offering
      Cost/contribution for each product
      Product life cycles
   b. *Raw materials*
      Source of supply and concentration
      Cost (variability, seasonality)
      Major suppliers (number, concentration, dependency)
      Contractual agreements
         specific terms
         cancellation penalty
         current backlog
   c. *Manufacturing process*
      Capacity at facilities
      Path of process: raw material to finished product
      Quality control
      Sub-contractors
      Backlog
   d. *Market for products*
      Recent growth and outlook
      Strategic plans and projection
3. **Marketing**
   a. *Sales force*
      Method of sales (direct vs brokers); review of all sales agreements
      Coverage

      Method of sales planning and forecasting
      Location and head count of staff
      Compensation of sales force
      Distribution channels

  b. *Advertising*
      Media types
      Budgets
      Use of advertising agencies

  c. *Pricing*
      Pricing policies and methods
      Terms of sale

  d. *Customer base*
      List of major customers and their volume
      Penetration of top customers
      Changes in customer composition
      Customer attrition rate
      Industries served
      Largest customers/degree of credit risk
      Contracts
      Seasonality/Cyclicality

  e. *Competitive position: advantages and disadvantages*
      Cost of production/distribution
      Uniqueness of products
      Reputation
      Relationships with customers
      Major competitors
      Competitive factors
      Indirect competition
      Potential for future growth in market or market share
      Risk of technological obsolescence

4. **Capital expenditures/research and development**
   Recent capital expenditures, last 5 years
   Planned capital expenditures, next 5 years
   Development of new products: history and typical cycle time
   R & D budget

5. **Facilities/equipment**
   Office or plant locations
   Owned vs leased
   Lease terms, renewal or purchase options
   Estimate of market value of facilities or lease
   Maintenance agreements
   Expansion capability/capacity utilization
   Proprietary equipment

Depreciation schedules and major equipment listing
6.   **Reporting and control systems**
Financial accounting and controls
Inventory measurement and control systems
Cost measurement
Production standards
Scheduling
7.   **Management**
Personal data on directors and officers, including references
Organization structure
Employment agreements and compensation
Incentive plans and fringe benefits
Retirement and pension plans
Reputation and morale
8.   **Labour**
Employee count by location and function
Cost of labour, including summary of hourly categories
Source of labour
Benefits packages
Union history: present and past
Labour agreements, if applicable
Labour relations
Personnel policies
9.   **Litigation**
10. **Patents, trademarks, copyrights and licences**
11. **Governmental regulation**
Health, safety and environmental issues
Import issues
12. **Pension and profit sharing plans**
13. **Contingencies**
Warranties
Product liability
Insurance (coverage levels and outstanding claims)
Disputed taxes
Contracts/obligations to be assumed
Off balance sheet liabilities
14. **Financial results**
a.   *Income statement*
Sales and margin breakdown by product
Cost of sales
Overhead and administrative expenses
Outlook for future, including sensitivity to recession
Discretionary expenses

b. *Balance sheet*
Working capital needs
Review of receivables (including ageing, concentration and bad debt history)
Review of inventory
Review of debt/term loans; copies of loan agreements
Review of prepaid and accrued accounts
Review of reserves and customer claims
Review of fixed assets (type, location, date of acquisition, recent appraisals)

15. **Miscellaneous financial data**
Forecast income statements, including major revenue and cash assumptions
Auditors' management letters
Tax audit status
Tax and book basis of assets/stock
Depreciation policies (book and tax) for capital assets
Other tax attributes, if any (NOL and ITC carry forwards)
Previously expensed assets still on books

16. **Corporate documents**
Articles of Incorporation, including all amendments
Bye-laws, including all amendments
Minutes of all meetings; both directors and shareholders
Samples of stock certificates, option certificates and any other outstanding securities

Table of Contents of Asset and Stock Purchase Agreements

TABLE OF CONTENTS: ASSET PURCHASE

Schedules and Exhibits

Schedule A   Real Property
Schedule B   Real Property Leases
Schedule C   Personal Property
Schedule D   Personal Property Leases
Schedule E   Inventory
Schedule F   Contracts
Schedule G   Accounts Receivable; Deposits and Prepayments
Schedule H   Proprietary Rights
Schedule I   Excluded Assets
Schedule J   Excluded Obligations
Schedule K   Allocation of Purchase Price and Assumed Liabilities
Schedule L   Seller's Financial Statements
Schedule M   Certain Change and Events
Schedule N   Litigation
Schedule O   Employee Pension and Profit-sharing Plans
Schedule P   Compensation
Schedule Q   Related Party Transaction
Exhibit A   Form of Opinion of Seller's Counsel
Exhibit B   Form of Opinion of Buyer's Counsel
Exhibit C   Form of Employment Agreement

TABLE OF CONTENTS: STOCK PURCHASE

Glossary

This section provides definitions of some of the more common words and phrases used in the acquisition process.

Acquisition   The process by which the stock or assets of one corporation come to be owned by another entity. The transaction may take the form of: 1) a purchase of stock, 2) a purchase of assets and an assumption of liabilities, 3) a reorganization, 4) a redemption of stock and a recapitalization, or 5) a merger.

Agent   (see 'Intermediary') A party authorized to act for either the buyer or the seller in the sale of a business. An agent arranges and negotiates transactions for a fee.

Allocation of Purchase Price   Assignment of the purchase price to individual tangible and intangible assets. Where a premium has been paid over the historic costs of acquired assets, acquirers often either 'step up' the value of tangible assets or apply a part of the purchase price to intangibles.

Basis   The historic cost of an asset. An 'adjusted basis' is the initial basis plus all additional expenditures minus the accumulated depreciation and all other direct charges.

Basket   A minimum threshold of claims which must be reached before any liability is triggered. Buyers seeking post-closing purchase price adjustments typically cannot make claims unless and until their total aggregate damages reach a specified monetary amount, or the 'basket'.

Book Value   Net worth. Assets less liabilities, as recorded on a company's balance sheet.

Boot-strap Transaction   (see Leveraged Buy-out) The acquisition of a company by a buyer with little or no equity capital to invest. The buyer purchases the target through the use of debt, thus pulling himself up by his 'boot straps' to buy the company.

Break-up Value   The value of a company's assets if sold separately, as in a liquidation.

Capital Gains   Profits from the sale of capital assets. The gain for tax purposes is based on the gross consideration received less the basis of the ownership.

Capital Structure   A company's net worth plus its interest-bearing debt, as recorded on its balance sheet. The capital structure is the 'foundation' on which a company is built.

Capitalization Rate   A rate (expressed as a multiple) applied to a company's earnings that reflects both its perceived risks and anticipated earnings growth.

Cash Flow   The excess of all cash sources less all cash uses. Often defined as a company's cash profit plus all non-cash expenses. 'Free cash flow' is defined as cash flow less all capital expenditures (ie, the cash that a company generates after all cash expenditures).

Closing ('Close')   The consummation of a transaction, when the conditions of a change in ownership are fulfilled and funds are transferred. A closing generally occurs simultaneously with the execution of a purchase agreement, though not always. A purchase agreement may be executed with a closing to follow, pending certain conditions being met.

Covenant Not to Compete   A covenant found in most purchase agreements, whereby the seller agrees not to compete with the business being sold for a certain period of time. To enforce non-compete clauses, courts have found that they must be specific in activity, place and time. Acquirers often seek to allocate a portion of the purchase price to a 'covenant not to compete', especially in circumstances where they are paying more than the net worth of a company's assets.

Covenants   In a letter of intent or purchase contract, an agreement to perform or abstain from performing certain actions. Covenants can apply to either party of a transaction, both before and after closing. A typical pre-closing buyer covenant would be to maintain the confidentiality of all negotiations. A typical post-closing seller covenant would be to agree not to compete in the same business for five years.

Disclosure Requirements   A full listing of disclosures required in any business combination involving a public company. Financial statements in such disclosures must conform to certain principles and standards.

Discounted Cash Flow   An approach to valuation based on discounting a stream of a company's future cash flows to their present value. The rate of discounting is determined by the relative cost of money and the perceived risk (and therefore, premium above the cost of money) inherent in the company.

Due Diligence   An examination by the buyer to confirm that the data provided by the seller is true, accurate and complete. Due diligence also refers to the auditing of the seller's financial statements and examination of the business and legal records. The period of 'due diligence' generally falls after a deal has been negotiated, but before the closing.

Earn-out   Additional payments made to sellers contingent on their meeting certain performance goals in the future. Earn-out payments are generally predicated on meeting certain sales or profit levels. Thus, the seller 'earns out' a portion of the purchase price.

Escrow   A 'hold-back' of a portion of the purchase consideration pending fulfilment of certain conditions. Generally, in acquisition matters, buyers demand that a portion of the purchase price be deposited in an escrow account for a certain period pending the outcome of contingent liabilities, such as collection of receivables.

Fair Market Value   The value at which an informed buyer will buy and an informed seller will sell, neither under any compulsion to do so.

FIFO   The 'First-In, First-Out' inventory cost accounting system. In inflationary times, FIFO inventories are often undervalued.

Finder   An individual who introduces a buyer to a seller for a fee. A finder is not an agent for either side; his role is merely to introduce.

Generally Accepted Accounting Principles ('GAAP')   Accepted accounting norms and conditions, as established by the Financial Accounting Standards Board (FASB) in the US and the International Accounting Standards Committee (IASC) in the UK and Western Europe.

Goodwill   An intangible asset, representing the excess of the cost of assets over their carried or market value. Goodwill is usually created by purchasing assets at a value higher than their fair market value. Goodwill is essentially 'air'; it represents nothing tangible, only the perceived value of the acquired company's business, reputation and anticipated stream of earnings.

Holdback   (see 'Escrow') The retention of a portion of the purchase consideration pending the outcome or fulfilment of certain conditions.

Horizontal Integration   The acquisition of other companies in an acquirer's existing field. A 'horizontal merger' is a combination of two companies which produce or sell the same goods.

Illiquid   Not readily convertible into cash.

Indemnification   The assurance by one party that the other party of an agreement will be protected from certain liabilities. In acquisitions, both buyers and sellers generally cross-indemnify each other. Sellers generally indemnify buyers against contingent or undisclosed liabilities; buyers indemnify sellers against claims by lenders or share-holders.

Instalment Sale   A transaction in which at least one payment of a note or other obligation is due at least one tax year after the close. In an acquisition of stock or assets, the gain (and, therefore, the tax liability) may be reported pro rata over the payment period, as payment is received.

Intangible Assets   Assets which have no material value. Intangible assets often appear on company's balance sheet as a result of an acquisition where the company paid more than the fair market value of the assets acquired.

Intermediary   ('Investment banker', 'Broker') An agent who acts for either the buyer or the seller in arranging a transaction. An intermediary is involved in searching for appropriate merger candidates, as well as negotiating and structuring the deal. An intermediary acts as a financial adviser to his client.

Internal Rate of Return ('IRR')   The compounded rate of return on an investment in an acquisition, including interest, dividends and capital gains, expressed in a per annum basis. The customary IRR expected by a senior lender is 8–15 per cent; the IRR commanded by equity investors in acquisitions ranges from 20 to 40 per cent.

Letter of Intent   ('Memorandum of understanding', 'Heads of agreement') A non-binding, written summary of the buyer's and seller's mutual understanding of the price and terms of an acquisition in the process of being negotiated. Since letters of intent involving public companies must be openly disclosed, transactions involving public companies often go right to contract, skipping the letter of intent stage.

Leverage   Balancing a relatively large load of debt on a relatively small equity base. To control significant assets through debt. A company with much debt and little equity is considered 'leveraged'.

Leveraged Buy-out ('LBO', 'Boot-Strap')   A transaction in which the stock or the assets of a company are purchased primarily through the use of debt. The acquiring entity borrows a substantial part of the acquisition cost against the assets or cash flow of the target company. The acquirer generally uses little or no equity capital in buying the target company, but rather anticipates repayment of debt through either the target's future earnings stream or a separate resale of the target's individual assets.

LIFO   The 'Last-In, First-Out' inventory cost accounting method.

Management Buy-out   A leveraged buy-out (see 'LBO') in which all or part of a management team buys its company from the shareholders.

Merger   A combination of two businesses into one. In a merger, Corporation A combines with and disappears into Corporation B.

Misrepresentation   False or misleading information provided to the other party to a contract.

Non-compete Clause and Non-compete Payment   See 'Covenant Not to Compete'.

'No-shop' Clause   An agreement in either a letter of intent or a purchase agreement which restricts the seller from either soliciting or engaging in discussions with other potential acquirers for a specified time period (usually 60–120 days).

Pay-back Period   The time required by a buyer to recoup his original investment in a company through its earnings. Generally, acquirers demand pay-back periods of between five and seven years, taking into account the time value of money.

Pooling of Interests   A method of accounting used in a merger, in which the balance sheets of two companies are combined. No goodwill is recognized on the surviving company's balance sheet, under the premise that no purchase ever occurred. The surviving company's balance sheet also retains the historic cost basis of all assets.

Present Value   The current value of a future payment or stream of payments. Such payments have to be discounted to compensate for the lost current income from, and the uncertainty of, the future payments.

Price/Earnings Ratio ('P/E ratio')   A ratio or multiple derived by dividing the total consideration paid in an acquisition (price) by the acquired company's earnings (either current or projected). P/E ratios are generated for comparative reasons, to test the relative cost of an acquisition against other like deals.

Principal   A primary investor in an acquisition; one who will hold most of the equity in the acquired company going forward. A principal is distinguished from an agent, who represents one side in a transaction for a fee.

Purchase Accounting   A method of accounting for an acquisition, in which a purchase price is allocated among the purchased tangible and intangible assets, with the remainder recognized as goodwill.

Purchase Agreement ('Buy/Sell')   A legally binding contract for the sale of the stock or assets of a company.

Recapture   The adding back to taxable income of certain items which were formerly sheltered from income, such as accelerated depreciation or investment credits. Selling fixed assets can often trigger a 'recapture' tax, allowing the government to 'recapture' taxes that would have been paid had the depreciation or credit not been taken.

Recourse   An agreement by a seller to recompense a buyer for the value of any assets that prove to not be worth their stated value. Recourse arrangements generally apply to the collection of receivables or the obsolescence of inventory.

Representations and Warranties   Binding claims by either party to a transaction. Both buyers and sellers generally warrant certain claims to each other: buyers that they are able to make the acquisition, and sellers as to the nature and condition of their companies.

Sellers' Notes   A note held by the seller to help finance an acquisition. Generally, sellers' notes are unsecured obligations, though they can be secured by a second lien on the assets or the stock of the company.

Senior Debt   Secured debt which has the highest preference to assets in a liquidation.

Stepped-up Basis   The result of increasing the basis of an asset from its historic, depreciated cost to one determined by an acquirer's cost or fair market value.

Subordinated Debt ('Mezzanine Debt')   Debt, often unsecured, which ranks below senior debt but above preferred and common equity in liquidation preference (hence the term 'mezzanine').

Synergy   The creation of greater value by combining two companies than previously existed when they were separate. This can be achieved through a combination of production or marketing skills, or merely a reduction of overhead and an elimination of redundancy.

Take-over   Acquiring a controlling interest in a target company, often without the consent of the target company's management.

Target Company   A company that has been selected by a potential acquirer as an attractive candidate.

Term Note   Interest-bearing debt which has a fixed date of maturity.

Vertical Integration   The acquisition of companies engaged in either earlier or later stages of production or marketing. The acquisition of either a supplier or a customer would be a 'vertical' acquisition.

Working Capital   The excess of current assets less current liabilities.

Index